ED UNDERWOOD

Author of *When God Breaks Your Heart*

A Tale about
Discovering God's Will

THE TRAIL

Tyndale House Publishers, Inc.
Carol Stream, Illinois

Visit Tyndale online at www.tyndale.com.

Visit Ed Underwood's website at http://edunderwood.com.

TYNDALE and Tyndale's quill logo are registered trademarks of Tyndale House Publishers, Inc.

The Trail: A Tale about Discovering God's Will

Designed by Jacqueline L. Nuñez

Edited by Danika King

Published in association with the literary agency of D. C. Jacobson & Associates LLC, an Author Management Company. www.dcjacobson.com.

Library of Congress Cataloging-in-Publication Data

Underwood, Ed.
    The trail : a tale about discovering God's will / Ed Underwood.
      pages cm
      ISBN 978-1-4143-9112-0 (hc)
  1. Hiking—Fiction. I. Title.
      PS3621.N3847T73 2014
      813'.6—dc23
                                  2014003273

Printed in the United States of America

20	19	18	17	16	15	14
7	6	5	4	3	2	1

To Dave Burchett, Kevin Butcher, and Don Jacobson,
honest followers of Jesus who express their love
by telling me the truth about myself and by
encouraging me to write a book now and then.

CONTENTS

CHAPTER 1
DOWNHILL RECKONING

Trust in the LORD with all your heart; do not depend on your own understanding. Seek his will in all you do, and he will show you which path to take.

PROVERBS 3:5-6

"*I REALLY HOPE* we're not driving up a dark mountain to meet some weirdo. Brenda, why did you talk me into this?" Matt rounded a sharp curve. He could hardly believe what he was about to do. "Couldn't we have decided without this guy whether we should move to Pasadena?"

Matt and Brenda had driven all night from Southern California to the Sequoia National Forest, east and north of Bakersfield. Every mile marker twisting along the narrow mountain roads intensified Matt's uneasiness.

It was only last Saturday morning they were sitting with Brian and Lindsey at Walter's Restaurant in their upscale neighborhood in Claremont, discussing a controversial topic—how to discover God's will.

After catching up with their longtime friends over breakfast, Matt had dived in, voicing the question pressing on his mind. "We're in the middle of a discussion over whether I should take this new position with an accounting firm in Pasadena. It would be quite a promotion and a lot more money, but when we try to talk about how to decide, it usually turns into a bit of a dispute. And you guys always seem so sure of God's will in your big life decisions."

Then Brenda had joined in. "It's just that Matt's so logical, so careful. His way of finding God's will leaves God out of it." She shot him a look. "He reads the Bible, but after that, it's all about facts, options, and reason. As if God's will can be found on a Quicken spreadsheet! But there has to be more to a relationship with God than that. If God really wants him to take this position—to uproot our family, move the kids to a different school, find a brand-new church—I know he'll give us some sort of sign."

"You sound just like Brian and me about three years ago," Lindsey said, moving her chair closer to the table. "Remember how we were trying to decide if we should move to a different neighborhood? I thought we should take the commonsense path, but Brian wanted to hear from God."

Matt had to voice his frustration at that point. "Come on, Brian. We're not asking God to guide us to the Promised Land, where all of redemptive history will occur. We're just trying to figure out if I should take this new job offer. If we're not breaking any of God's commandments, he wants us to use our own logic to decide."

Brian took a deep breath. "Are you personally satisfied with that view of knowing God's will?"

"No, not at all," Brenda said. "It's as if God isn't even there."

Matt was silent.

"We know a guy who can help," Lindsey said. "Three years ago, we began hearing some stories about a special pastor named Sam. We got in touch, and he asked us to meet him up in the mountains for some kind of retreat. It was too weird for me at first, but Brian insisted. So we did it. And it changed our lives."

Brian put a hand on Matt's shoulder. "You need to meet with him. We'll watch your kids for a couple of days. Just trust us on this."

So Matt and Brenda had spent the last forty-eight hours preparing to follow an old fireman-turned-pastor they had only met on the phone into the wilderness of the High Sierra. The clerk at REI helped them find all the equipment the old man had instructed them to buy: backpacks, sleeping bags, necessities for the trail, and pairs of boots Sam had told them to "break in right."

As he now steered around another hairpin turn, Matt thought out loud. "We know everything about breaking in our boots, but we still don't know anything about this holy man of the mountains. I still can't believe we agreed to this crazy scheme, Brenda."

He could hear the fear in Brenda's voice when they turned right at a sign marked Limestone Campground. "This is really out of the way, Matt. Are you sure we're supposed to turn here? This road doesn't feel like it leads anywhere, and it's so steep."

Matt reached for her hand. "Brenda, we both knew this was going to get bizarre. You saw the sign, and this is where the GPS says to turn. It may be a mistake, but I think we should follow through on our decision. I'm doing my best here—I've never been up a road like this either."

"I'm sorry, Matt. I'm just afraid."

"Me too. The best way you can help me right now is to watch the road and pray."

"O Lord, please let us know if you want us to keep going. If you want us to turn back, give us a sign."

"Come on, Brenda. Please don't bring that up right now. You know I don't trust your 'signs from God.' Could you just pray for protection?"

"Okay. I will admit that safety is our number one priority right now." She began to pray again. "Father, please protect us on this road and from this so-called pastor if he really is a weirdo."

There was silence. They continued driving up the mountain road in the dark.

Matt looked at the clock. Fifty minutes until their rendezvous with Sam. He mentally considered the options before them, analyzing every pro and con until he was certain he was prepared to answer Sam's questions. Should they uproot their lives and move to Pasadena to see what God had in store for them in what he knew was an awesome opportunity? Or should they stay in the only home and school their children knew and the church they all loved? They had to decide—Claremont or Pasadena—and Sam had promised to teach them eight principles for discerning God's will for their lives.

When they arrived at Blackrock Ranger Station, they found an old man sitting on the tailgate of his white Toyota Tacoma 4×4 reading with a flashlight like he was waiting for them on his front porch. They got out of their SUV to stretch, and the man closed his book and walked over to them with a smile. He wore an old pair of Levi's, a khaki shirt over a T-shirt, and a ball cap. Every part of him seemed efficient, though he walked with a noticeable limp. "I'm Sam Lewis. Welcome to the high country."

Matt shook Sam's outstretched hand and got right to his concern. "I'd like to ask a few questions about this, ah, expedition we're on here."

Sam turned his light onto their boots. "Looks like you broke your boots in just like I asked. That's important. You'll never make it up here with blistered feet, and Casa Vieja Meadow is two steep downhill miles from the trailhead." He looked up at the anxious couple. "Sure, what do you need to know?"

Matt spoke as respectfully as he could, but his risk-assessing accountant mind-set kicked in. "For starters, are you sure about this? I mean, we just met you. Have you ever been here before? We can't even get cell reception. What if something happens, like a twisted ankle or worse?"

A faint swish of some creature came from the dark woods. Brenda moved closer to Matt.

The old man ignored the sound. "Yes, I have been here before—I used to work around here, and I've been walking into the Golden Trout Wilderness for over forty years. That's why I wanted to meet you here. It is remote, but that's part of the deal. I need your full attention if this expedition, as you call it, is going to work. I'd feel better if you thought of it as an adventure."

"Is this where we start hiking?" Brenda asked with a friendliness that surprised Matt. "What were you reading? I can't make out the title."

"It's the New Testament, but in Greek. I've been studying Galatians lately." Sam seemed apologetic for being caught reading the Bible in an ancient language. "The trailhead's about fifteen minutes north. Fill your canteens here and then jump into your rig and follow me."

On the way to the trailhead in their SUV, Brenda voiced her thoughts. "I like him. He's not a weirdo, but he is a little weird. He reads Galatians in Greek but calls a car a rig. How did you know he meant our Nalgenes when he said 'canteens'?"

"War movies." Matt concentrated on the road, made visible by the headlights. "That's what they used for carrying water back in the day. He's old school. This may be a bust, but at least it's going to be interesting."

He couldn't help remembering Lindsey's parting words from that morning at Walter's. *"It felt like a huge risk following Sam into the high country. But I'll never go back to the old way of trying to live without knowing God's will."*

◢

Sam led the couple single file down the trail through the towering trees. With liturgical precision, he'd laced up a pair of scarred, ten-inch leather boots he referred to as his "White's," then shouldered a pack and picked up his weathered hardwood hiking pole. Behind him walked his opposites: husband and wife outfitted in the finest REI had to offer, stepping lightly, obviously in shape, the way a tennis pair walks onto a court. Headlamps on, they chose their footing carefully, following the path in the shadows of the breaking dawn. Sam told them not to worry—it would be much easier to navigate the trail in the full light of day.

Sam stopped abruptly before a bridge in the little meadow where their journey would begin, and Brenda nearly walked into him. He pulled a water bottle from his pack, took a few swallows, and shrugged his shoulders forward to adjust the load. He wiped his mouth on his sleeve, set his canteen on a rock, and bent to fuss with the brace on his right knee. As he straightened up, careful to grab his water on the way, he griped under his breath and then took a few more swallows.

"Brenda, would you mind putting my canteen into that little thing on the back of my pack? Arthritis—just can't seem to get my hands to work the way they did in my prime," Sam explained. "So, what do you think? Nice country, isn't it?"

Matt stepped forward, clearly agitated. "So, Sam!" he said. "Please at least tell us where we're heading. This is all a little out of the box for us." The young man stepped closer, forcing himself into Sam's line of sight. "You haven't shown us a map; you don't seem to have a GPS or even a compass. I like mountains as much as the next guy. This may indeed be nice country, but it feels like dangerous country to us. You assured us that this would be a place where we could hear from God!"

A blue grouse exploded from a nearby lady fern, protesting their presence as she gained altitude. Matt jumped, and Brenda yelped. When they'd recovered, Sam said, "Well, now that he has your attention, what do you think God's telling you?"

The young man gripped the trekking pole in his right hand tightly and pounded it on the first wooden plank of the bridge. He visibly pulled himself together, then said, "This is just one old wooden bridge in the middle of a meadow in the High Sierras. And that big chicken bird was just startled. It probably does that twenty times a day. I was afraid of this. It's a bridge on the trail that happened to be where some bird spent the night—nothing more, nothing less.

"Instead of trying to figure out what the flight of a stupid bird means God is telling us, we should be thinking about what other wildlife might be watching us right now. How will an encounter with a bear or a mountain lion help us decide whether or not to take a job in Pasadena?"

Sam had been looking closely at Brenda's face while Matt spoke. He saw her eyes drop in disappointment and resignation. In that moment Sam knew two things for sure: first, that this was about a lot more than a new job in Pasadena; and second, that it was not going to be possible to avoid hurting these two in order to help them.

"On the contrary, Matt." Sam stepped back from the trail, tucked a thumb in his belt, and swept the other hand toward the wilderness below. "I believe that down this trail is your only hope for learning how to make decisions with the confidence that you're in God's will. I'm not going to lie to you. I've seen both cougar and bear on this plateau. But the meanest critter up here is the old range cow. That's what we'll be watching out for."

Matt looked confused and fearful. "Sam, have you heard anything I've said? I'm just looking for some answers here."

"I can't force you to do this. If you want to go back, now's the time to decide. It's only a thirty-minute climb back to the rigs. Once we dive off from here, we're committed, and it's going to take us the rest of the day to get to camp and set things up. The night falls dark and quick." He pulled a large blue handkerchief from his pocket, wiped his face, and tied it around his neck. "You think you're uneasy now, try spending the night along the trail without a fire—"

"Sam?" Matt interrupted again.

"Yeah, Matt? What do you want?"

"What do you mean that down this trail is my only hope for learning how to find God's will? Why just me?"

"Well, Matt, you're a professional, an accountant who's used to figuring things out and managing the risks of your options. That's what you're trying to do right now—manage your risks by controlling the situation. You felt foolish when that old blue grouse made you jump. You hate feeling out of control, and you manage your life with knowledge. You're constantly calculating, incessantly trying to understand so that you don't make a mistake. I can see it in your eyes. This is hard for you because you don't know anything about this trail, these mountains, hiking, or backpacking."

Sam looked him in the eye and waited.

Matt took a deep breath, and his shoulders dropped. "I'm not trying to control this. I only want to understand what we're doing here on this bridge in the wilderness with a man we've just met. That's not control; that's gathering information. I just want to understand. What does following you down this trail have to do with finding the will of God?"

"I already told you that," Sam said. "You need to walk this trail in front of us because this place—this wild and beautiful plateau—is where God chose to take you beyond your understanding to trust, beyond control to faith. You live in a world of understanding—your understanding. God's asking you to follow him, not me, to a world where he can guide you, a world beyond your understanding, beyond your control. A world where you're out of management options, a world where you trust him or fail. And this is that world. The high country, big country, mean country, you-gotta-trust-in-someone-bigger-than-yourself country."

Sam was stern and motionless. "The high country humbles a man, Matt. And that's what you and I need more than knowledge. Humility."

Matt's face pinched in on itself. "I've always depended on God's Word. If I can't understand why we're here, then I'm not taking another step. I don't care what you say. You're asking for a lot here, Sam."

"The heck with what I say." Sam looked sharply at him. "Is that a Bible in your pocket? Pull it out and turn to Proverbs 3:5-6."

Matt closed his eyes. "That's one of my favorites. I memorized it when I first met Jesus."

"Then quote it for me." Sam pulled his own backpacking Bible from the left pocket of his khaki shirt. "Better than that, let me refresh your memory.

"'Trust in the Lord with all your heart,'" Sam said from memory as he turned to Proverbs. "These aren't my words; they're God's words spoken through the wisest man who ever lived, a man who dedicated his life to understanding the world around him. It took Solomon a lifetime to figure out that even he was too weak, sinful, and stupid to manage his own life. If you don't believe me, read the book of Ecclesiastes.

"'Trust in the Lord with all your heart,'" he started again. "'Do not depend on your own understanding. Seek his will in all you do, and he will show you which path to take.'"

Sam looked off, trying to retrieve a memory from his personal studies and notes.

"That phrase—'he will show you which path to take,' or 'will make your paths straight' in some translations—is a Hebraism, a figure of speech that shows God setting you on the best path possible, the path he himself has prepared for you. It's like being on the freeway of God's direction rather than losing your way trying to read your own map on streets of your own choosing."

He handed the Bible to Matt. As the young man looked over the passage and Sam's notes in the margins, Sam said, "What it says in whatever language you want to read it in—Hebrew, Greek, Latin, or plain English—is this: the opposite of faith is control. God doesn't need your strength to guide you, but you do need to trust his strength to recognize his guidance. It's your trust, not your strength.

"Think about your life, Matt. When do you feel closest to God? Is it when you understand everything? Is it when you're in control? Or is it when you know that if he doesn't show up, you're sunk? Is it when you feel personally strong or when you realize how strong he is?"

Matt nodded, relaxing his stance. "I remember meeting

Brenda on campus the day I told God I was going to end a long relationship that wasn't honoring to him. I opened the door for a group of ladies, and there she was. I feel closer to God when I'm relying on him."

Sam looked intently at Matt. "That's what he's asking you to do right now, right here, on this bridge. Rely on him, regardless of what your controlling heart may be screaming. If you want to experience God's guidance, you must go beyond understanding to trust."

Brenda mouthed the words *beyond understanding to trust.* A look of hope had come into her face when Matt spoke about the moment they'd first met.

"You're not in management, Matt," Sam said. "You can't control this. If you want to discover God's will up here or down in the flatland, it's going to take faith. Because—and I'm going to say it again—*it's your trust, not your strength.*" Sam hiked his right shoulder and rolled it forward. "Old army injury," he explained. "Talk about not being in control, try jumping out of a perfectly running airplane. Now that's a picture of the faith God's asking you for: the faith a jumper has in his parachute. If the parachute fails, you're toast. And still, all you have to do is land wrong one time, and there you go. Gimpy shoulder for the rest of your life."

Matt handed Sam his Bible and looked at Brenda.

Brenda stared at the place in the trees where the grouse had disappeared. Her eyes squinted in the brightness of the sun breaking through a stand of cedar. Thoughtfully, she said, "God's telling us that we have to cross this bridge if we're ever going to know what he wants us to do. It's a sign, a test."

"A reckoning, maybe?" Sam shifted his weight, turned, and looked at the young couple to see if they had heard him. He pushed his hat up and back to make eye contact. "Next stop, Casa Vieja Meadow."

Under the bridge, the creek cut through the rushes, sedges, and grasses, running cold in its golden-hued bed. To the east, the trail ran parallel to it, a steep ribbon of powder-white decomposed granite through the tangled manzanita and towering red fir, ponderosa, and Jeffrey pine. From camouflaged pulpits high above the trail, blue jays blared and tree squirrels chirped the general alarm, alerting every creature of the wilderness to the presence of newcomers.

Sam stood on the bridge for a moment, lost in reverence— for the mountains of his youth, for these semitrusting fellow hikers, and for his God. As always, a quiet fell on the trail here, a quiet heavy with tales and memories of lost hikers, lightning storms, forest fires, bear sightings, timber rattlers, and spooked horses. Just past the clearing ahead, the timber closed in on the trail, diving into the beauty of the Kern Plateau.

Golden trout darted from the shadow of the bridge as Sam's White's clumped heavily on planks worn smooth by those who had gone before. "No fresh tracks," he said, studying the clearing on the other side. "We may have Casa Vieja Meadow all to ourselves when we get there tonight. I wonder if the cowboys have brought their stock in to graze yet."

Brenda and Matt followed him, Brenda stopping briefly to snap a picture of the view behind them. "Is that where the mean cows and bulls come from?" Brenda asked. "How does a cow get up here, anyway? And are they all mean?"

Sam stepped carefully across a rotten plank in the bridge. "Watch yourself here." He turned to ensure they didn't fall through. "No, most of them just don't want to be bothered. If you meet a mean one, you'll know it."

"Maybe you ought to point them out to us," Matt said from the rear. The young accountant's interest in what Sam had to say had evidently increased. As they walked along, he said, "You promised to teach us eight surefire principles for discovering God's will. When are we going to start writing in the brand-new Mead journals you insisted we bring with us?"

"Class is already in session," Sam responded. "First lesson comes from Proverbs 3:5-6. As soon as we reach the campsite, you'll want to initiate that journal. You tell me what the first principle is."

"I'm not in management." Matt repeated Sam's words, a smile in his voice. *God doesn't need your strength to guide you, but you do need to trust his strength to recognize his guidance.*"

The filtered light of the rising sun glowed bright on yellow and purple wildflowers to the left and right of the path before them. An eagle screeched, and a coyote moaned in protest after an unproductive night of hunting. The pine boughs high in the timber whished in the morning breeze.

In that moment before they walked off the bridge, only Sam heard the still, small voice of God in the sounds of the wilderness. He stepped forward and squinted into the sunlight on the plateau. "I have a feeling we're all going to need God's strength before this is over."

CHAPTER 2
LEFT OR RIGHT

The LORD's loyal followers receive his guidance.

PSALM 25:14 (NET)

THE TRAIL OPENED suddenly along the lupine-lined banks of the spring-fed creek. The hikers came upon a meadow, a long, meandering mixture of high-country grasses and wildflowers, with fingers extending north and east and a rectangular fence lining the borders of the flat middle. The creek ran steadily from the east down the center before dumping steep and swift into the south fork of the Kern. Pine and fir lined the edges, like forest sentries halted in ranks to see what God could do in these unshadowed acres. And Sam knew God wouldn't disappoint.

Matt and Brenda moved into the meadow with the slow, deliberate steps of subjects before the throne of a sovereign. "This is . . ." Matt tried to explain the moment. "This is . . . I mean . . . What I'm trying to say is, this is . . . I don't know what to say."

Brenda reached into her pocket for her camera. "Stop, Matt. Wait, I have to get a picture of this. It's like the mountains in *The Sound of Music*, only better. Way better."

Sam walked past them and pointed to the left. "Those are some nice alpine peaks to the west, way out there past the last ridgeline. Sun's out and it's all sparkly. He's braggin'."

Matt squinted his eyes. "Who's bragging?"

"God." Sam pulled his map out of his pocket and folded it to center Casa Vieja Meadow in a six-inch square. "See, here's where we're standing. Right where the red dashes of the trail hit that white spot. That's it—Casa Vieja. The guard station's right there just up from the meadow, straight across. We're going to make camp east of the station some and up in the trees. There's a spring up there nobody knows about. Not on the map, but it makes for a nice camp." Brenda smiled at Matt, and Matt nodded in agreement. Sam handed Brenda the map. "From now on, you're the map reader of this expedition. The only thing left to do today is set up camp and decide whether we're going to turn right or left from the west end of the meadow tomorrow morning."

They turned east to follow the fence line. Brenda patted the folds out of the map and turned it to keep the fence posts on her left. "Is this north?" she asked, pointing to the cabin across the meadow.

"You're a natural, young lady. You just oriented your map. Tonight I'll show you how to really orient your map, only it won't be a cabin but God's own heavens to guide you."

"Why are the wires down on the ground?" Matt asked.

"Cowboys haven't brought in their stock yet. These fences are to keep the cattle from overgrazing the grasses of these meadows. If you take care of 'em—and the cowboys do—they'll last until Jesus comes. But you don't want to leave the barbed wire up during the winter. The cold's so deep the wire snaps. When the cows graze the meadow down some, the cowboys'll just pull up the wire to keep 'em out of this easy grass and force them up into the stringers."

"What's a stringer?" Brenda asked.

"Like a finger of the meadow extending up into the timber. Like that one right over there." He motioned across the flat. "That's the one we need to navigate to now. Our camp's on an old trail up out of that stringer. See it on the map, Brenda?"

"Yeah. It looks like there's a bridge across the creek if we take this trail."

"Good girl," Sam shouted, and *Good girl* echoed across the meadow.

The three walked the width of the main meadow and stopped at the base of the stringer. Sam caught his breath, pulled up his handkerchief from his neck, and wiped the sweat from his face. "Before we climb up in the timber, I need to explain your options. In the morning we'll break camp, walk to the west end of the meadow toward those peaks, and then you'll have to choose."

The couple peered into the west. "The trail forks left and right. If you turn left, you're on the trail to Kern Flat, where you can catch some big rainbow trout. If you go right, you're on the trail deeper into the wilderness toward Tunnel Meadows and walking along creeks full of golden trout."

The anxiety came back into Brenda's face. And Sam could tell Matt was already analyzing this choice to go left or right.

Brenda studied the map. "Well, this is all new to us. We'll trust your judgment. You decide. Matt just wants to fish some, and I'll be happy either way as long as I can work on some scenes in my sketchbook. They both sound exciting to me. What do you think, Matt?" She shifted her weight, and Sam noticed she was favoring her right foot. "It feels like I may have a blister."

"Listen, you two," Sam said abruptly. "This is all about you learning how to find God's will. When I say you have to decide, I mean you have to decide which way God wants you to go. He either wants you to go left and down or right and up, but not both. And it will be him telling you which way to go, not an old man in a pair of White's."

The couple appeared taken aback by Sam's intensity. "Are you telling me that we're supposed to find God's will for which way to turn on a mountain trail?" Matt asked, skeptical.

Sam pulled his cap down over his eyes. "That's exactly what I'm saying."

"You mean if you were by yourself you would walk to this point on the map—Show me where that is, Bren. You would get up in the morning and turn left or right believing that you were choosing God's option for you?" Matt pressed.

"Yes. I'd turn left or right with unshakable confidence that God is guiding me to his good and perfect will, his best horizon."

Brenda looked nervously at Sam. She turned to Matt and touched the map with her right forefinger. "It's this fork in the trail."

Sam's heart caught signals his ears couldn't hear. He'd felt Matt's resistance as soon as he had started talking about going left or right, maybe even before he spoke the words. But Brenda seemed willing to try. Sam wanted to leap to her defense and tell Matt to give this a chance, and he wanted to resolve their tension right there. Years of experience told him that he had to wait for God to do something, but he was afraid for Brenda, and for Matt, too.

"She's got it. And it's your decision but God's choice." Sam nodded quickly to Brenda. He stared squarely at Matt. "Well, I'm walking up this stringer to unload my pack and make camp. Brenda, you need to get out of those boots before you rub a blister." He turned toward the trees and began heading off. "Your decision but God's choice, kids. But you have to decide." He muttered under his breath and looked back. "By tomorrow morning!"

*

Brenda watched Sam walk away.

"Wow, where did that come from?" Matt said. "I was just asking. Did he actually say 'kids'?"

Brenda remembered Lindsey's warning that Sam would call

them kids. She also knew why the memory had made Lindsey smile. He meant no harm; it was just his way. She looked cautiously up the hill to make sure the old man couldn't hear her. "That's the man we asked to teach us about this," she said quietly. "Sam's passionate. He's lived a lot of life. He's followed God, and he's confident."

Matt's lip trembled. "Listen, Brenda," he rasped. "I never said he wasn't confident or even godly, okay? I don't know what he wants from me. I'm just trying to get some answers." He sighed. "This is so frustrating to me right now."

Brenda hesitated. "Matt, I love you, but it's just like Sam said this morning. You need control. You call it an honest question, but Sam's like a lot of us who feel there's more to life than just gathering information. He lives knowing God will tell him what to do. He must be tired of arguing with Christians like you who are afraid to admit that God could actually tell them which way to turn. Some of us like the idea of being on God's trail instead of our own. And wouldn't you? In your heart of hearts?"

"Sure," said Matt. "I'm here, aren't I? But this seems like it's more personal between Sam and me."

Brenda didn't have to wonder how to find the unmarked campsite without Sam. All they had to do was walk toward the racket the old man was making in the still woods. "What could he possibly be doing to make so much noise?"

Sam's pack leaned against a log by a circle of rocks. Brenda imagined the stones had been arranged carefully over the decades by lonely trappers, cold hunters, and tired cowboys. Next to the fire site was an impressive woodpile. Before they could ask how a man Sam's age could cut so much wood so quickly without an ax, Sam slammed a dead pine limb from the forest floor against a young fir tree, and it exploded into three-foot-long pieces.

"Set your pack next to mine, Matt. And help me set in enough wood for tonight's fire and breakfast tomorrow. Brenda, take off those boots, and maybe cool your feet some in the spring. You can hear it bubbling up just past that little cedar." He came toward them. "Legend is that this site was developed by a packer named Honus Jonus. Never could prove it one way or the other by my research. Bold name, though, Honus Jonus. It's quite a place, isn't it?"

Brenda and Matt looked cautiously around the surprisingly developed campsite. "It seems that way," Matt said quietly. "If it's all the same to you, Sam, we'll unload our packs up there on that flat place in the shade of that tree. Seems a great spot to set up our tent."

Sam grunted. "Not there. Not under that ponderosa. Too dangerous with all those dead limbs up high. Just put 'er down next to the log like I said, and help me with this wood."

Brenda squirmed at the tension and shifted her feet nervously, watching Sam's weathered face, his narrowed eyes, his determined stare.

"Why is he fighting me on this, Brenda?" Matt said under

his breath. "I can't see any difference between that tree and a thousand others we've walked by today." Brenda gave him a pleading look, and thankfully Matt paused. His voice dropped almost apologetically as he addressed Sam again. "I don't want to fight with you over this, Sam." But then he turned back to Brenda. "Bren, let's just unload our packs up there for now." He stiffened and marched uphill in a slight crouch.

The young woman was embarrassed, but she waited until Matt was well up the hill. "Matt's pretty headstrong," she said softly to Sam. "He's faced with a lot of responsibility at work. He's smart, and he's confident."

"Well, let him be smart and confident," Sam said. "He's not much of a listener. But I'm guessing you already know that." He turned toward the fire ring, rubbing his right shoulder. "Go ahead, girl. Do what he says. You two need to talk and make your choice about tomorrow's hike. I'll wait for you down here."

Sam met her gaze once more, his eyes sorrowful. "I can't do this for you, Brenda. It's up to you and Matt to discern God's choice: left or right." And then he became earnest. "You need to know that I like Matt. I like his spunk and his commitment to the Bible. But this is going to get messy, and I'm sorry for that."

Brenda smiled and surprised herself when she reached up to rub his cheek with her hand. "That's all I can ask, Sam. Thanks."

Matt's voice came from above. "Brenda, bring your pack up

here. I think you're going to like this campsite. It's nice and flat, and the view is spectacular." She headed up the hill.

*

Sam filled his mind with warm memories of this place, trying to ignore the hushed conversation between his two companions, back from their hilltop campsite. He rearranged the rocks around the fire pit, whistling, of all tunes, "I Saw Her Standing There" by the Beatles. The couple laughed quietly as he fussed with the stones.

Matt walked to the log next to the fire ring and sat down. He picked up a stick and pushed pine needles around in the dirt. Brenda perched next to him.

Sam bent to set his camp stove next to the log, then took a seat on a nearby boulder. "Did you two decide which way God's leading you? Are we going to Kern Flat or Tunnel Meadows?"

The wind stilled and the mountain took a deep breath. A brood of chipmunks chattered and chased each other uphill.

"You mean did Brenda decide," Matt replied. He sounded resigned, ashamed, and agitated. "I hardly ever see God's hand in decisions like these."

Sam ignored his tone. "At this point very little depends on the ultimate destination, although God does know where he's guiding you. His hand isn't as much in the choice of turning left or right as it is in reaching deep within the condition of your heart. That's where Sam's first rule of theology comes in: God is smart. He knows the type of Christian who will recognize his guidance—the all-in-for-Jesus believer, the sold-out disciple."

Matt looked up from the pine needles. "Like when God was leading the Israelites to victory over Goliath and the Philistines, and only David the shepherd boy could see it. David had been trusting God to protect him against wild beasts—a lion and bear, I think. He was ready to appreciate the Lord's guidance because his heart was right with God."

"That's a perfect example from the Bible of what I'm talking about, Matt." Sam leaned forward and smiled. As he did, Matt's shoulders relaxed some. It was, Sam thought, a good sign that some of the young man's stubbornness was coming from a good place—his reliance on the truth of the Scriptures.

"God isn't concerned with turning left or right? He's smart?" Brenda broke in. "You said God would tell us which direction to go, and that's the choice we discussed up there on the hill. You didn't say anything about a rule of theology."

"That's the second of the eight secrets to discovering God's will," Sam answered.

"Are these the same eight secrets you told Brian and Lindsey about?" Matt asked, sounding curious.

"That's right," said Sam. "We already talked about the first one: *God doesn't need your strength to guide you, but you do need to trust his strength to recognize his guidance.* It's the under-girding truth for finding God's will. Still, in most people's minds, the next step is trying to find the destination God is leading them toward. Too often you get people looking out-side of themselves to find the path God wants them to walk. But when we read the Bible, we learn that we need to ask ourselves what God's seeing inside of us before we start asking him to guide us. When God reveals his will to a heart that isn't inclined toward him, that heart will miss the message because it's not looking for the truth. A person like that just wants their own way."

Brenda leaned forward and threw her arms up. "But you told us that God had a specific will for us to turn either left or right tomorrow morning. That seems pretty outside of ourselves to me. Doesn't this bring us right back to the idea that we won't know where to turn when the time comes?"

"No!" Sam shook his head. "It never happens like that. God makes it clear what our responsibility is and what we should look for inside ourselves to recognize his guidance."

"Okay, just how does he do that?" Brenda sounded betrayed.

Sam realized she must think he was taking Matt's side in the debate over God's willingness to tell a Christian exactly what to do. "Relationship," he said with a smile.

Sam began to explain. "Once God has my heart, I'll be receptive to his guidance, and he knows I'll choose his will. His specific will for me hasn't changed, but my heart has changed. Now I'll be able to discern whether he's turning me left or right."

He grabbed the Bible he had set on the ground and leafed through the stained pages. "Romans 12:1-2 sums it up perfectly.

After eleven chapters on the mercies of God, Paul makes his main point." He read slowly.

> "And so, dear brothers and sisters, I plead with you
> to give your bodies to God because of all he has done
> for you. Let them be a living and holy sacrifice—the
> kind he will find acceptable. This is truly the way to
> worship him. Don't copy the behavior and customs
> of this world, but let God transform you into a new
> person by changing the way you think. Then you will
> learn to know God's will for you, which is good and
> pleasing and perfect."

Sam rested the Bible in his lap. "English translations differ, but in the Greek text it's clear that much of the book of Romans is connected to discovering the will of God. 'And so,' or 'therefore,' says Paul, 'in view of God's mercies,' or 'because of all that he has done for you.' The Greek preposition there is *dia*, I think." Sam looked down the hill, trying to recall the word. "Anyway, I know it looks back at all that comes before—all those mercies we don't deserve. Paul goes on, 'present your bodies to God.' That means give him control of your life, Matt. Then Paul uses an interesting word: *logikhn*. That word has a dual implication of worshipful service and reasonable decisions. We get the word *logical* from this.

"So what he's saying, kids, is, 'Make the logical choice to

worship him by giving your life to the Merciful One.' Finally he connects all of this to God's will by saying that if we'll do this, we will discover the will of God by 'testing' or 'experience.' And not just some ordinary view of God's will, but it gets emphatic. His good, pleasing, and perfect will."

The wind rose while Sam talked, driving small late-afternoon clouds across the sky. Their shadows moved over the campsite. The treetops sang harmoniously in the wind, made modern melodies and hummed ancient songs.

"Now that's a lot to take in sitting on a log in the Golden Trout Wilderness, and I'm sorry to get so technical on you. Still, it's the core New Testament truth, I believe, on discovering God's will. It's all about relating to a great God. Only those who present their lives to him because they trust his mercies can know his good and perfect will. And that's a decision that means looking inside. Only you and God know if you're trusting his mercies enough to give him your heart."

"We read the book of Romans last year in women's Bible study, but I totally missed that connection," Brenda said.

"I've always wanted to learn how to read the Bible in its original languages," Matt added. "Do you have any other verses like that?"

"Of course," answered Sam. "I've spent a lot of time in the Psalms. Initially it surprised me how many times the writers of the Psalms ask God to show them his will or talk about knowing his will. I did a study years ago I titled 'The Guidance Psalms.'

What impressed me most was the emphasis on relationship. These psalms aren't as much a how-to-know-his-will manual as a how-to-know-him guidebook. Those psalmists understood that God will not be manipulated by the impatient demands of his people. Neither does he offer magical formulas guaranteeing his blessing. Instead they viewed their paths as being more brightly illuminated as their trusting relationship with him deepened.

Sam turned left in his Bible, stopping at the Psalms. "King David's worship leader, Asaph, wrote these words in Psalm 73:28: 'But as for me, how good it is to be near God!' This guy Asaph sounds like a real God's-will-finder to me. He was a Romans 12 believer before Paul ever lived. He knew that his first priority was nearness to his God. The biblical model for knowing God's will centers on relationship."

Brenda gave a frustrated sigh. "I thought you said that God reveals his will to Christians. This sounds like you're saying just trust him and serve him, and forget about finding his specific will. Then I don't know why we're up here. Let's just go back home and serve God."

Matt chuckled. "Sounds biblical to me. Our responsibility is to be faithful. After that, God only continues to guide us through his Word and our *reason*." He emphasized both syllables.

The breeze whistled louder in the trees, howling its counsel for all high country creatures below and for all those humans who would sometimes visit there.

"That's not what I'm saying at all, Matt." Sam moved his head from side to side. "Romans 12 invites us into deep relationship, the relationship of an all-in believer, the one who has given his or her life to God. That's his revealed will for every Christian—to be all in. *The question isn't 'Does God guide Christians?' but 'Are you the type of Christian who would recognize his guidance?'*"

Sam studied his open Bible, absorbed. "Once we're sure that 'all-in' is true of us, then we can move forward with the confidence of knowing that we're the type of Christian who can discern God's guidance. Here's my main verse for this secret to knowing God's will: Psalm 25:14. Just like in Romans, you're going to get some differences in the English translation here. But the literal Hebrew says, 'the advice of the Lord belongs to those who fear him.' I take *advice* as a synonym for *guidance*. And the Hebrew concept of fearing the Lord meant trusting him enough to do what he says, to be loyal to him. So I would put it like this: 'The Lord's loyal followers receive his guidance' (NET). This is David's way of saying God guides his all-in people."

Although the young couple surely had a basic understanding of God's omniscience, Sam suspected they had never heard anyone connect what God knew about the heart of a person with the effectiveness of his guidance—or heard that while God loves and guides all of his people, it is his loyal followers who benefit most from his guidance.

A sudden wind stirred the trees high above Honus Jonus

camp. The sound of cracking wood and the thud of a heavy limb sounded from just up the mountain. The three of them spun around and stared at the two-hundred-pound limb driven into the forest floor above them from the momentum of its fall. Sam watched as Brenda turned to face Matt. Matt was frozen to the log, gazing at the pine spear now marking the site where he had wanted to pitch their tent.

"Look, Matt! This isn't a battle of your will against Sam's. I'm scared. You're going to have to listen to this man." Brenda struggled against tears. "I've seen you in situations like this before. You were trying to show him how brilliant and self-confident you are. Well, up here none of that matters. He's just trying to help us, but he can't if you insist on playing your power games."

Matt's eyes revealed his own fear. "I didn't want anything like that to happen," he said defensively. "Sam, you should have explained why you didn't want us to put our tent up there."

Sam got up and went over to Brenda to put his arm around her shaking shoulders. "Widowmaker. The Forest Service warns backpackers against trees like that, but every year somebody's killed because they just have to camp in the shade of a half-dead ancient pine like that one that just let loose. They know better than the experts. It's a waste of time trying to teach and protect a person like that. They're too smart to listen, too smart to recognize guidance." He thought for a moment. "That's what I'm talking about. God himself could tell a person not to camp under a widowmaker, but if that person doesn't trust him enough to do what he says, he'll have to face the consequences."

Matt still stared at the place where he and Brenda had dropped their packs. "That was close. We could have died. You should have convinced me." He clenched his teeth. Sam walked quickly from Brenda's side, stood before Matt, and put one hand on each of his shoulders.

"It would have been a waste of time," he repeated softly. "Down in the valley you're smarter than most, Matt. But up here you're stupider than most. Smart and wise are two different things. A wise man is smart enough to admit when he's stupid. The high country humbles a man, Matt."

Seeing the fear in the young man's eyes, Sam said, "You have to give your heart to God, son. Not in theory, as the God who might have something good for you if you're interested, but in reality, as the God who is smarter than you and wants your heart more than your performance."

The young accountant looked uncomfortable, very uncomfortable. "Get used to feeling stupid," Sam said, breaking the awkward silence. "Comes with the territory. Nobody ever discovered the will of God by being smart." He backed away.

Brenda took a picture of the pine spear between their packs, and Sam glanced toward her. "Speaking of pitching tents, we better get busy. Chew on that awhile. God is smart and efficient. He knows who is going to listen to him and who isn't. The question isn't 'Does God guide Christians?' He does. The question is 'Are you the type of Christian who recognizes God's guidance? Are you all in for Jesus?'"

Sam paused. "That's the second secret. 'The Lord's loyal followers receive his guidance' is your reference—Psalm 25:14 (NET). *Make sure you're all in for Jesus.*"

The sun shone through the trees, casting a hazy triangle that settled on the circle, and the wind whipped up a small whirl of cold ash from fires past.

CHAPTER 3

IN OR OUT

Search me, O God, and know my heart; test me and know my
anxious thoughts. Point out anything in me that offends you,
and lead me along the path of everlasting life.

PSALM 139:23-24

SAM HAD TOLD BRENDA that early evening was the most peaceful time in the high country, and he was right. Everything was calmly subdued but not yet dark. Brenda and Matt, their tent now pitched, walked next to Nine-Mile Creek, and even when the path narrowed, they stayed next to each other. A mountain bluebird perched on a fence post turned and acknowledged their presence. For a moment the clearing was soundless, and then Matt spoke with quiet intensity.

"Brenda, I may be a jerk at times, and I may not agree with your ideas about how God works in our lives, but I honestly want to be all in for Jesus," he said. "Please give me credit for at least that—for trying to be all in." He stopped and took her hands in his. "I want our relationship with him to define our lives."

Brenda looked up at him sweetly. "Matt, you are the love of my life and an attentive husband and father, and when a problem is in your sights, you are incredible. You don't waste time and money on shallow hobbies and pursuits even when you want to relax, and you don't run from the hard things of life. You are not like anyone else I've ever known. People seek you out for advice, and your advice is almost always right because of your deep understanding of the Bible. It's a shame I don't understand you sometimes. But I have no doubt that you want to be all in for Jesus."

She kept standing in the shadow of her husband, waiting for him to say something. To her surprise, he bit his quivering lower lip and tears spilled down his face. "Right now, at this moment, I don't care if God ever tells us where to live or work."

Brenda could see his face warm with emotion, and she could almost feel him searching for the next sentence. "He's already told me what's most important," Matt said. There was fear in his voice. "Baby, I wish I were the man you just described, and I want to be that man. It's just that . . . I mean, what if . . . ?"

Matt paused. His face, which seemed to show a fight going on inside him, turned the color of ash. Brenda couldn't help being afraid.

"Matt, what are you trying to say?"

Her husband took a deep breath. "Brenda, I want to be a better man, for you and for God. I mean . . . I love you, Brenda. I'm just reeling from all of this right now."

Brenda couldn't ignore the unsettled look on Matt's face. It had once been a rare expression for him, but lately she was noticing it more often. She assumed there was a problem with some client at work. But now she wondered.

The orange of the sunset shifted east across the meadow and lifted to the skies as the sun sank in the west behind falling ridges. Dusk came to Casa Vieja, a cool twilight over the Kern Plateau. A big red-tailed hawk circled overhead, screeching haunting warnings to establish its authority over the skies.

In the loneliness of the meadow, the young couple walked hand in hand like newlyweds back toward the stringer and Honus Jonus camp. But Brenda had never seen her husband cry, not even at their wedding, until that moment next to the creek. It felt like a breakthrough, and maybe it was. But a breakthrough to what?

They stopped to get their breath in the thin alpine air. Matt looked out over the meadow. "When do you think Sam is going to ask us about our decision? I feel like he needs to know that this new job means a lot more money and is really a dream come true for me. Except for moving so far away from your parents and our neighborhood. And it took us so long to finally find a church. Those are the questions I want to ask Sam tonight."

"I'm glad we came," Brenda said.

"Me too. I'll let you give Sam our report." Matt smiled as they began to climb up the stringer. "I've been talking too much. We want to be all in for Jesus. No question in our minds. You tell him that, Brenda."

A couple of hours had passed since they'd left camp. Brenda shuddered and felt cold, although the sun had just gone down.

✧

"You kids hungry?" Sam knelt next to an inviting fire. "Coffee's on and the beans are just about ready. I'm fixin' to throw these steaks on. Hope medium rare's good for you. I hate turning a good steak into charcoal." The flames crackled in protest when Sam stirred the coals. Sam unwrapped three rib eyes and threw them onto the grill, which was supported by rocks under all four corners. He pushed them together over the coals, and the fire blazed when rendered fat sizzled from the meat.

"Love a good steak the first night on the plateau. Besides, it's not too bad coming in, so the extra weight doesn't count much, even for a gimped-up old pastor far north of his prime." He smiled at their surprise and almost unconsciously nudged the steaks around the grill with the corner of his left boot.

Brenda watched him from the other side of the fire. "I like mine well done."

"Well, if I were still young and stupid I'd make you eat it medium rare. I remember too well the day I made my daughter gag down bloody steak just because I thought it wasted meat to burn it. I'd trade all of my tomorrows for that one single yesterday."

Sam looked up to smile his apologies to Kris Kristofferson for stealing his line. His modesty was lost on the couple. Under his breath he whispered, "'Me and Bobby McGee.'"

He stood and stared into the fire for some time. "If I could live that day over, I would; but that's not how life works. If she were talking to me today, I would cook her meat so well done she wouldn't see a molecule of blood or fat. I would cut it up for her and tell her how much I love her and that she's more important to me than any old cut of meat. I would order her a side of beef for her freezer and fly to Philadelphia to cook it for her special, just the way she likes it, because she's my special girl." Sam caught himself, and his voice faltered before he choked out in nearly a shout, "So you got it, girl—I mean, Brenda. One burnt-to-a-crisp rib eye coming up, just for you."

It was almost dark now, but the fire illuminated the trunks of the trees on the edges of the campsite and the stars twinkled alive against the black alpine night. "This is the most beautiful view I've ever seen," Brenda murmured. "Even more incredible than the cathedrals I visited in Europe." She walked slowly and timidly around the fire until she stood next to Sam. She took a deep breath as he continued to worry over the steaks. He was barely aware of Brenda so close to him.

"Sam," she almost whispered. No response. "Sam!"

"Oh, sorry, Brenda."

"I'll have that one in the middle." Brenda pointed to the smallest steak. "And, Sam, thank you for cooking it through.

Matt likes his medium rare, just like you. We've had some battles over that issue too." She knelt next to Sam and looked through the darkness toward the meadow. "Sam, we want to be all in."

"I know."

Brenda stood up. "You know? Then why did you ask us to take that walk in the meadow and think about it?"

"Something being true of you isn't the same thing as you *knowing* that it's true. I knew you wanted to be all-in-type believers. Why else would a busy young couple drop their lives for a few days and drive this far to a place you've never even heard of to hear what some old man had to say about God?"

Matt walked over from his and Brenda's tent with their two headlamps. Sam looked quickly and intently at him, then turned back to Brenda. "There are a lot of Christians just like you and Matt who want to be all in for Jesus but haven't connected that commitment with knowing God's will. Remember, we're talking about relationship here. An all-in believer is one with a relationship-oriented heart. They want more of God, and God, consequently, gives them more. Like you, they're just stumbling forward with commitment in their hearts, but sometimes they forget that it all begins with God's mercies. I'm thinking that the two of you had a moment down there by the creek. And that's a good thing, a God thing. He loves it when his children love him enough to go all in for his Son."

"Well, we did," Matt volunteered with an abruptness Sam didn't trust. "Have a moment, I mean." The young accountant fixed his lamp around his head and handed the other to his wife. "So," he said, "helping Christians see the importance of devotion to God is a key to discovering his will. But what comes next? I still don't know what this has to do with whether we turn left or right tomorrow morning. Or, even more important, whether or not I should take this job in Pasadena."

Sam avoided the invitation. He had sensed Matt's momentary vulnerability and his knee-jerk return to a more linear conversation. "Our steaks are ready. Matt, grab a couple of plates over there on the log. I turned the stove off under the beans."

They sat by the fire after dinner. Sam undid his big blue handkerchief and used it to grip the coffeepot handle. He poured coffee into three tin cups, then handed one to Matt and gave another to Brenda. From his back pocket he brought out a spoon and passed it to Brenda with two packets of sugar and one creamer and winked. "Matt told me this is how you like it." He blew on his to cool it some and gestured with his cup. "Now that you're on your way to being all in for Jesus, the next secret to finding God's will is receiving his real-time guidance."

Sam noticed that Matt had pulled out his journal and pen, like a student ready for class to begin. "Write down these three words: *trust*, *relationship*, and *intimacy*. Intimacy with God is where we're going next, and your passage is Psalm 139."

Matt set his notebook aside and picked up his Bible, flipping to the middle. "Oh yeah, I studied this just last year at a prayer breakfast. Isn't it the psalm about God's omniscience, him knowing everything?"

Sam motioned with his cup again. "That's part of it, Matt. But it's so honest and vulnerable, I'd hate to categorize it so theologically. These are King David's meditations on what God knows about him, but notice that they begin and end with David saying something to God about his heart. What is that?"

Matt read slowly, his face tensed in concentration. When he stopped, he picked up his cup, took a sip, and swallowed. "He wanted God to examine or search his heart," he said, and Sam heard the nervousness in his voice.

"That's right." Sam recognized the fear in Matt's eyes and suspected the young man had a secret. "Correct. David is inviting God into the deepest folds of his soul. What does he go on to say at the end, in the last two verses?"

"'Search me, O God, and know my heart; test me and know my anxious thoughts. Point out anything in me that offends you, and lead me along the path of everlasting life.'"

Sam smiled. "'Lead me along the path of everlasting life.' That tells me it's a guidance psalm sure enough, kids."

Brenda swallowed her coffee hard and held up her hand like a stop sign. "Slow down a little, Sam. I'd like to know what comes between the beginning and the—"

"—end." Sam finished her sentence. "And I'm sorry. It's a bad habit I have, running ahead of myself to make a point."

The night seemed more inviting now that Brenda had

spoken up, and Sam went on. "I've preached it and taught it so many times I have the outline in my head. Three questions followed by three requests. But you're right, Brenda. Will you read it for us?"

Matt held his Bible between them, and she read in the light of her headlamp.

"O LORD, you have examined my heart
and know everything about me.
You know when I sit down or stand up.
You know my thoughts even when I'm far away.
You see me when I travel
and when I rest at home.
You know everything I do.
You know what I am going to say
even before I say it, LORD.
You go before me and follow me.
You place your hand of blessing on my head.
Such knowledge is too wonderful for me,
too great for me to understand!

I can never escape from your Spirit!
I can never get away from your presence!
If I go up to heaven, you are there;
if I go down to the grave, you are there.
If I ride the wings of the morning,

if I dwell by the farthest oceans,
even there your hand will guide me,
and your strength will support me.
I could ask the darkness to hide me
and the light around me to become night—
but even in darkness I cannot hide from you.
To you the night shines as bright as day.
Darkness and light are the same to you.

You made all the delicate, inner parts of my body
and knit me together in my mother's womb.
Thank you for making me so wonderfully complex!
Your workmanship is marvelous—how well I know it.
You watched me as I was being formed in utter seclusion,
as I was woven together in the dark of the womb.
You saw me before I was born.
Every day of my life was recorded in your book.
Every moment was laid out
before a single day had passed.

How precious are your thoughts about me, O God.
They cannot be numbered!
I can't even count them;
they outnumber the grains of sand!
And when I wake up,
you are still with me!

O God, if only you would destroy the wicked!
 Get out of my life, you murderers!
They blaspheme you;
 your enemies misuse your name.
O LORD, *shouldn't I hate those who hate you?*
 Shouldn't I despise those who oppose you?
Yes, I hate them with total hatred,
 for your enemies are my enemies.

Search me, O God, and know my heart;
 test me and know my anxious thoughts.
Point out anything in me that offends you,
 and lead me along the path of everlasting life."

"'Do you appreciate my circumstances?'" Sam began. "That's the theme of the first five verses and the first question. Answer? Well, of course he does. His knowledge of my circumstances couldn't be more exact. It's overwhelming.

"Question two is in the next section. Look again at the next six verses. 'Are you near?' Answer? He's everywhere. We couldn't get away from him even if we tried.

"Third question on David's mind is, 'Do you understand me?' Well, in the following six verses David lets us know that this is an absurd question when we consider that God formed us in the womb and he's preoccupied with thoughts of us.

"Finally, three requests in the last five verses: deliver me;

search me; guide me. That phrase 'the path of everlasting life' literally reads, 'the reliable ancient paths.' This tells me that the same God who knew all about me before I was even conceived knew the path he wanted me to walk after I was born."

*

Matt looked again at the page. He wondered if David had really wanted God to search his heart. He wondered if he could ever pray that prayer and mean it. He wondered why Sam chose that psalm and asked him to consider the first and last lines. Matt remembered the men's Bible study group reading this same psalm, but nobody had even suggested that it was about God's guidance. Matt had been there, talking freely with the other men, with no idea of how uncomfortable David's words could make him.

"I still don't understand," Matt whispered. "How does this help me decide about a job in Pasadena?"

All the passion in Sam came out then. "I like to think of it as a circle and a dot. The real-time part of this is to make sure that we're within the circle of his revealed will for us, his will for every Christian regardless of specific life situations. We open ourselves up to God's examination by being totally honest with him and with those who love us, and he lets us know if we're outside of that circle."

Sam grabbed the stick Matt had been doodling with in the dirt that afternoon, pushed the pine needles left and right, and drew a circle with a dot near its inside edge. Matt and Brenda looked down, shining their headlamps on it. "I believe that 90 percent of knowing God's will is staying within the circle of intimacy by genuinely opening our lives up to his examining Spirit. That is, 90 percent of your really important guidance will come from staying within this circle of God's revealed will for every believer."

"There you go again, Sam," Brenda interrupted. "You're moving too fast. What do you mean, 'God's revealed will for every believer'? Is that when God gives a Christian a sign or a feeling that lets us know it's him?"

"Not yet, Brenda." Sam dropped to one knee and looked up. "That comes later. I'm talking about God's will for *every* believer—the part of God's will that is universal, meaning that whether you're a Christian in Cambodia or California, this is something that God wants you to do."

"Wait," Matt said, sitting up straight. "This is where the Bible comes in. You begin with the Bible, God's Word."

Sam looked him in the eye and smiled. "That's why we call it revelation. The Scriptures reveal God's will for every believer. And that's where we begin, all of us. So we only think about the other 10 percent—the dots of his more personal will—after making sure we're in the circle of his general will for every believer, following the teachings of the Bible. Of course, once we're sure we're in the circle, we should strive to determine the 10 percent—that is, the next step he's guiding us toward. It's real-time. 'God, please let me know if I'm in the circle.' If I'm in the circle, then I go with my heart and trust him that I'm on the dot."

Matt shook his head. "Go with my heart?"

"Yes, go with your heart," Sam said. "After you've prayed David's prayer. 'Examine me, according to all that I know from your Word.' Your redeemed heart will want to do what the Bible teaches, Matt. But as you and I both know from personal experience, we can read something in this book and do exactly what it says not to do."

Matt couldn't speak. He looked away into the darkness.

*

Once again Sam felt the fear in Matt's heart.

Brenda stood and walked to the tent. "Wait until I get my camera," she said. "I want to hear this."

She returned and stood over the circle and the dot, preparing to take a picture in the ambient light of the fire. "Point your stick to the dot, Sam."

Sam smiled and gave an awkward laugh. "I don't need to be in this picture, but I'll humor you, girl."

After she took three pictures, Matt's attention came back to the circle and the dot. "Seems simple." He continued in a confident voice. "I think we understand the importance of relationship and staying within the circle of his revealed will. So is finding God's will just making sure that you know what the Bible says about a certain choice?"

Sam shook his head. "No. Turn out your headlamps and look up. Now, can you see where I'm pointing? That group of stars that looks like a dipper?"

Brenda was delighted. "The Big Dipper. My dad used to teach me the constellations. Right there, Matt." She reached to guide his hand up and to the right. "Start up there at the handle and trace it down through the dipper. Do you see it?"

"Oh yeah, I see it. Seems obvious now that you've pointed it out."

Brenda went on. "Now, the stars of the Big Dipper are the same brightness as the North Star. The last two stars of the dipper are called the pointers, right, Sam?"

"You keep talking, little girl." He paused. "Excuse me for calling you 'little girl.' Keep talking, Brenda. I'm getting a lesson here too." Sam hoped she could tell he was pleased.

"Okay, Matt. Loosen up a little. Why are you so tense?" She shook his elbow. "Now imagine a line through the pointers and follow it up to the star shining about as bright. That's the North Star! The Big Dipper rotates around the North Star all year long, so the pointers may be pointing down or sideways, depending on the season."

Sam interrupted. "But knowing where north is won't help you at all if you don't know where you are on the map! An' why? Because . . . because if you didn't know you were just up out of this stringer, coming out of this meadow, next to this spring in this wilderness, your only choices would be to walk north till you hit the north pole, south till you hit the south pole, or east or west until your hat floated."

Sam stood up and paced, gesturing in the firelight. "You have to know where you are on the map, where you're starting from." He looked at Matt. "God's Word, his revealed will for all of us." He stared into Matt's face. "But God won't begin to guide us north, south, east, or west unless we start from where he wants us to start: the circle of intimacy with him that only those who have opened themselves up to his Spirit know. So his first directional guidance is always to honestly and openly step into the circle of intimacy."

"How does he do that—show us if we're in or out?" snapped Matt.

Sam sat down and rested the stick in the dirt, and then his eyes teared, blurring the light of the fire. "When I was a young father, I knew I had a problem with my daughter that needed to be solved, but I didn't know what to do. The daughter I just told you about—she's a surgeon in Philadelphia now. She was running hard into adolescence, and it felt like she was rebelling against every value we stood for. Around others I did a great job of acting as if we had this happy family, but my rage against her was what you might call our family secret. As I look back on it now, I was firmly denying that my personal pride had anything to do with the conflict. I'm sure the Spirit was urging me to examine myself, to search the Scriptures to see if I had any fault in the equation. Like the fool that I was, I kept thinking that she should apologize first.

"Finally, at the desperate urging of my wife, I called a Bible teacher I greatly admired. When he answered the phone, I said, 'Prof, my daughter won't respect me and I'm trying to figure out God's will on how to deal with it.' As I began to explain, he interrupted me. 'Sammy,' he said, 'this isn't about your daughter's disrespect of you but about your disrespect of God.' Then he didn't say anything. Silence.

"I didn't know what to say. I eventually mumbled, 'But how am I disrespecting God?'"

Matt looked at Sam in surprise. Sam hoped the young man would see that he was not the only one who'd dealt with a secret.

"'Sammy,' my old teacher said, 'if you're telling me you can't think of one way you could love your daughter better, then the only place to begin is by making sure that you're not grieving or quenching God's Spirit. You do remember those commands, don't you?'

"Sure, I knew them. Paul's letter to the Ephesians warns us not to grieve the Spirit by doing something he's telling us not to do. And in 1 Thessalonians Paul tells his readers not to quench the Spirit by failing to do something he's urging us to do. What did that have to do with my daughter's disrespect? I didn't get it.

"When I asked that, he said, 'Sammy, restate your problem in intimacy terms between you and God.'

"'Intimacy terms?' I shot back. 'What do you mean, intimacy terms?'

"'I mean,' my professor said, 'that I don't want to hear

about only the shortcomings or behaviors of your daughter. Tell me what is happening between you and God in grieving and quenching terms.'

"I still didn't know.

"'Then how can you possibly know God's will for any area of your life, especially the difficult and painful aspects of parenting? You're wasting my time,' he barked."

Brenda held her cup out for more coffee and Sam reached for the pot. He produced another two packets of sugar and one creamer, and she stirred them into the cup as he poured. She looked up at Sam and smiled. "Did he call you 'kid'?"

The old man laughed and pointed the pot toward Matt.

"I've had enough coffee. What did you say after that?"

"I just held the phone to my ear." Sam returned the pot to the fire. "This didn't sound like my beloved professor at the other end. He graciously and mercifully broke the silence.

"'If you can't tell me if you've grieved or quenched the Spirit,' he said, 'you aren't going to receive God's real-time guidance. You're just complaining about a painful situation. God only reveals more of his will to those who are responding to the guidance he's already offered.'

"Being a student of the Bible, I suddenly realized I knew how I was grieving God's Spirit in my relationship with my daughter. After I told Prof, he asked a few clarifying questions. Then he said, 'What are you going to do about it?'"

Sam nodded toward Matt and said slowly, "This is where

you connect what you know from the Bible to your life. Matt, like you, I was in love with the Scriptures, but I had to make it about my life to go deeper with God. I said, 'I'm going to confess it and claim 1 John 1:9, that if we confess our sins, he is faithful and righteous, forgiving our sins and cleansing us from all unrighteousness.'"

Matt poured the rest of his coffee onto the fire, and steam went up, hiding him.

Sam kept talking. "My professor wasn't letting me off that easy. 'That's a great beginning,' he said. 'That's the honesty God's grieved Spirit is looking for, but if you just confessed to God, would you be able to say that you're not quenching his Spirit any longer? That is, would you be able to honestly say that you have done everything his Spirit is asking you to do in this situation with your daughter?' he asked.

"'No,' I said."

Sam could now see Matt again, and his head had dropped. Sam paused a few moments, then went on with his story.

"'Then you have a flawed plan for discovering God's will,' he told me. 'What is that hard action the Spirit is prompting you to take in this precise area where you want guidance—your relationship with your daughter? And don't give me some Christianese pabulum here. I mean in your most honest heart of hearts. Only when you have turned to God with that kind of trust—abandoned trust that does what he says and trusts him for the results—will you receive his more specific guidance. That's called repentance.'

"I thought about it for a few minutes and said, 'For some reason I've had a few Scripture verses on my mind lately. It seems as if I should apply these to my relationship with my daughter, but I've hesitated because I just can't figure out how that would make this better.'

"He said, 'That's the point of repentance, isn't it? To turn to God in trust rather than continuing to trust in your own resources and plans? You're starting to get it. Not until you trust him completely with your daughter—even to the point of admitting how wrong you've been—will he guide you more specifically in your leadership of her.'"

The night was deepening, and the moon was rising behind the ponderosa and fir that circled their camp. Sam noticed that Matt had looked up when he said the word *repentance*.

"That was the day I let God's Spirit begin to guide my relationship with my daughter, the day I started admitting that my pride had a lot to do with the conflict. But it was way too late for her. I wish I could say that my repentance erased the wounds I had put on her soul. It didn't, but it did open my life to the real-time guidance of God. It forced me to take that first honest, Spirit-led step into the circle of intimacy concerning his will for me in loving my little girl. I learned that my responsibility was to do everything I knew to stay within the circle of his will for our father-daughter relationship. Not just what I was reading in his Bible, but also what his people in my life—like my wife and my professor—were saying to me. Then, and only then, would he begin to reveal the 'dots' of his more specific will."

Sam stood painfully. "The idea is, now that you've agreed that you're all in for God, you need to say what David said in Psalm 139. 'You know everything about me, Lord. *Search me, and know my heart.* Tell me if there's anything in me that's straining this relationship. Am I grieving or quenching your Spirit in any way?' My experience with the Holy Spirit is that he's really good at answering that request.

"So here's your third secret to discovering God's will: *Stay within the circle of intimacy with God, and trust him that you're on the dot of his good and perfect will.* Write it down in your books before you turn in. Psalm 139:23-24 is your Scripture: 'Search me, O God, and know my heart; test me and know my anxious thoughts. Point out anything in me that offends you, and lead me along the path of everlasting life.'"

Sam watched the couple closely. "Now, here comes the hard part. What are we to do if the Spirit points out something that offends God?"

Brenda didn't hesitate. "Confess the sin and repent."

"That's right. Confess it; agree with God that what he said about your sin is right and that you are wrong. Repent of it. Turn to God in abandoned trust, no matter what the consequence."

Matt didn't respond.

Sam waited. "Matt, do you agree with that? That you need to step back into intimacy with God by confessing and repenting?"

He looked at Sam for a moment. "Yes."

"That's enough for tonight, kids," Sam said. "I'm worn out. We can pick this up tomorrow morning at breakfast. It's going to be nice sleeping tonight. You two turn in and talk this over. First with God and then with each other. I'm going to stay up a bit and let this fire die down some."

~

As Brenda zipped her sleeping bag to her shoulders against the chill mountain night, she was struck by the simplicity of what she had heard. Sam's teaching was so simple she'd missed it until now. *Stay within the circle of intimacy with God, and trust him that you're on the dot of his good and perfect will. Stay within the circle, and trust that you're on the dot.* After all, why would you want to follow a God who didn't know you or a God you couldn't be honest with? And why would he reveal his guidance to you if you didn't want to be near him?

Brenda yawned and prayed, telling God how much she wanted to be close to him. *It's been a long time since I talked to you this way,* she prayed. *I'm not sure of all the reasons you brought us up here with this old man. But I'm sure that part of what you had in mind was to remind me of how much you want me to be close to you. How did David put it? "Search me, O God, and know my heart." That's what I want, Lord. Right now I want to be intimate with you way more than I want to know whether you're guiding Matt to take a job in Pasadena. Search me, O God, and know my heart.*

She turned to Matt. "You're unusually quiet, Matt. What are you thinking?"

From the darkness, Matt whispered, "Brenda, can we just go to sleep?"

"Of course," Brenda said. "I love you, Matt."

"Me too, Bren. Me too. . . . You have to believe that."

They fell asleep that night in Casa Vieja Meadow. The Milky Way glimmered against the black sky overhead.

CHAPTER 4
NOW OR LATER

For everything there is a season, a time for every activity under heaven.

ECCLESIASTES 3:1

SAM SAT NEXT TO the morning fire like an old dog at his master's side. From a rock he and an old firefighting buddy had wrangled out of the draw decades ago, he could look out over the ridge lying south toward Blackrock Saddle and trace the trail they had walked in on. It was a nice view, full of memories good and bad—but mostly good.

Sam reminisced for a moment. He thought about the first trip here with two firefighting friends, his body lean and his life before him. Then he thought of when he brought his bride and daughter to this very spot, and he was saddened. He looked at the name at the top of the list carved into the ponderosa on the edge of camp: *Katie Lewis*.

And Sam could remember that day: her curly hair, green

eyes, and that smile when she was still his special girl and they were buddies. He wished he'd known then what he knew now, what he'd told Matt and Brenda the night before about God's will and living in the circle.

Although there was morning brightness on the ridge, under the trees daybreak was heavy with the haze of dew. Through the thin walls of Matt and Brenda's tent came the occasional coughs and whispers of a couple waking up, and now and then the sound of voices raised or hushed in heated discussion.

Brenda unzipped the door and emerged from the tent in tears. Matt reached out to grab her ankle, but she pulled away. She didn't look over at Sam and walked off in a pair of flip-flops. Matt immediately followed, barefoot and grimacing with each torturous step across the forest floor.

Sam poured a cup of coffee and turned off his camp stove under the simmering oatmeal. "Looks like the secret's out, Lord." The morning winds blew down canyon, stirring the fine dust and ashes around the fire. Sam covered the oatmeal and prayed.

Sam was in his tent packing his gear for the trail, stuffing his sleeping bag into its sack, when Matt bent into the doorway. Sam pulled the cords tight and waited.

"Sam," Matt said, "do you think you could finish getting breakfast ready while we get dressed? We need your help, and it has nothing to do with discovering God's will. It's serious. I've really messed up."

"Breakfast will be ready in fifteen minutes. Don't be too sure this isn't about finding God's will. That's serious too. Life is serious, Matt. All of it."

They took places across from each other around the fire, but Sam did not serve the oatmeal. He tossed a handful of twigs on the fire, and the young couple flinched in surprise at the crackling noise, so he stopped. Stillness descended on the camp again. A few minutes passed, and then a few more. Matt sat in silence, staring at the flames. Brenda gazed at him for a moment, then looked down at her boots.

"Matt has a girlfriend," Brenda said. The couple looked quickly at Sam.

"Had a girlfriend," Matt corrected her. "Had a friend who was female. But it wasn't an affair. We didn't have sex. It was inappropriate and wrong. But she's a colleague, and she was going through a tough divorce. I was just trying to help her, and then . . ."

Sam gripped the serving spoon tightly and studied their faces. The stillness was in their midst once more.

Brenda burst out, "And then he got involved. He was totally absorbed with her emotionally. They worked out together; he took her to lunch, met her for coffee. They even took drives to the beach so they could talk for hours about her life and her problems. They took drives to the beach, Sam! Did you walk hand in hand on the beach, Matt?" For a moment she continued to stare at Matt. Then her eyes moved slowly down to her boots again and she wept, softly and desperately.

Sam stood to step over Matt and sat next to Brenda, putting his arm around her. "Young man, this is what it feels like to receive God's real-time guidance. Right here, right now. The Spirit is heavy and powerful around this fire."

Matt said, "It's a fascinating idea. And I'm willing to receive his guidance, but maybe I've missed something. Why is this about guidance and not about my sin?"

Sam's hand shook as he pointed the serving spoon toward Matt. "Don't you see?" he cried. "David's plea, 'Search me, O God, and know my heart,' gives you a choice. It makes this the most important guidance moment of all. This is your in-or-out moment, your God-given opportunity to step into the circle. It throws the decision right back on you. For if you can grieve the Holy Spirit—and you did—it is also true that you can confess and turn to God in abandoned trust. That's repentance. And up to now, all this debate about turning left or right out of this meadow or working in Pasadena has been secondary to what God was really doing in your life: forcing you to admit your sin and turn to him. You need to step back into the circle, son. Don't you see?"

*

Matt began to feel the weight of the moment. He looked at Sam and Brenda and saw how, with them, time had already stopped. He remembered Sam's teaching on Psalm 139 and that David had asked God to test him and know his anxious thoughts so that God could lead him. When Matt thought of the agony of trying to manage his secret, he could feel again his fear of being found out, and he longed for peace. He had told himself that at least he hadn't committed adultery, but he knew he was living in a lie. Always the heaviness of his sin was upon him; always the fear of losing his marriage and his family. Could this be what Sam was talking about? Could it be that this was God's way of protecting him from an even more serious expression of his sin and rebellion?

"Yes, I see. I . . . I do see. But what comes next? Now that my sin is out, how do we move forward? I've made such a mess of things."

Sam's eyes were sympathetic now, his face relaxed. "What comes next is breakfast," he said. "And then I'm going to clean up and get all of our packs ready for today's hike while you three work this out."

Matt clenched his hands, and his right heel pumped nervously. "Three?"

"You, Brenda, and the Holy Spirit. This is what I was talking about last night. You've grieved the Holy Spirit, just like Paul said in Ephesians. It was the Spirit who made you miserable because of your sin, and it was the Spirit who brought you up here."

Sam stood up. "I need to talk privately with your husband, Brenda. Trust me." He took Matt aside, leaving Brenda next to the fire.

"Be careful not to get all analytical. This isn't an accounting problem. You had a secret sin against God and your wife. You asked if God could guide you to Pasadena and God said, 'No, not until you step back into the circle of intimacy with me by getting honest with her and me.' What you're about to do is hard, so take as long as you need. Remember what Jesus said about asking the forgiveness of those you've sinned against and what John said about being honest about your sin in 1 John 1:9. It takes more courage than intelligence to repent. You're both going to have to trust God with this mess if you ever want to move forward together."

Sam began to speak in a lower pitch, and his sentences slowed. "Speaking of moving forward. Once you're inside the circle, you'll be able to know something with a confidence that was beyond you when this secret was between you and God. You'll know you're following the dots of his good and perfect will. And those dots are either leading south to Kern Flat or north to Tunnel Meadows."

Matt and Sam returned to the fire. Sam looked into the faces of the couple and smiled. "Let's eat."

A gust of wind from the west whistled through the tops of the trees. The pine boughs flexed up and down; the dry, brown pine needles on the ground sailed a few feet. As quickly as it had come, the wind died, and Honus Jonus camp was quiet again.

They ate their breakfast quickly and without words. Sam pulled his Case knife from his belt and studied the ground, soon finding a small limb to whittle. It looked to Matt like he was making a toothpick. The couple cleaned their dishes mechanically and walked away. Matt could feel Sam watching them go.

About a hundred yards from camp, Brenda stopped and looked off into the cloudless blue sky.

Matt kept his distance and put his hands in his pockets. "Well, what do we tell Sam? Left or right? As if it matters anymore. This is insane. I just confessed to the worst mistake I've ever made in my life and I'm supposed to care which way we turn on a mountain trail?"

"Mistake? You did a bad thing, Matt. But you seem more angry over Sam asking you to make this decision than aware of how much you've hurt me. You keep thinking about what you've lost and what you would do if you were in charge. Couldn't you just listen once and at least pray about whether we should turn left or right?"

Matt's face hardened, and he pulled a quarter from his pocket. "How about I do this? I'll flip a coin. Heads, we go left; tails, we go right."

He looked over at his wife, whose eyes were closed as she slid down the trunk of a tree and sat hopeless in the dirt.

"I'm sorry, honey. I'm sorry. I shouldn't have said that. Okay, okay. Let's pray. Whatever you want. Just, please, could we talk about what really matters here?"

She didn't answer.

*

There was a stack of wood shavings on the ground at Sam's feet by the time Matt and Brenda returned to camp.

Brenda's expression was hard, and she knew that her eyes were red. Matt walked behind her but at a distance. She didn't look back. "I guess we're going to turn right, Sam." Brenda knew this was a stab in the dark. After what she'd learned about her husband's betrayal, how was she supposed to hear God's guidance for this decision? And Matt hadn't even tried.

The old man sheathed his knife, rounded the bill of his hat in his hands, and put it on. He looked at the two weary pilgrims, picked up his pack, and shouldered it. "Saddle up. Tunnel Meadows it is."

The sun was directly above by the time they were halfway to Tunnel Meadows. Brenda felt the blister on her heel, and she knew her heart wasn't in this hike. The exchange with Matt had drained her. Scenes of him and that woman together haunted her thoughts.

There was little conversation as they walked, and the stillness of the afternoon was on the trail. Even the voices of the cowboys behind them and the bark of what Sam said were the cow dogs in the roundup seemed muted to Brenda against the sound of her heart pounding. The air was thin, and the extended climb over the ridge to Beer Keg Meadow overwhelmed Brenda. Near the rock outcropping left of the summit, she saw a marmot chirp its alarm and then dive out of sight. Around the last turn of their descent down the other side of the ridge, they hit a large creek. Sam dropped his pack and walked back to Brenda, still only halfway down the slope. She shrugged her pack and put her hand on Sam's shoulder, wincing with every step. She knew she was done for the day, and Sam carried her pack to the creek.

The clear, cold pool of Long Canyon Creek was still in the late afternoon. The sun had burned hot on the trail as they'd hiked along, and mountain hues of green and brown glowed in the light. But by the pool among the scrubby manzanita, a nice shade prevailed.

It was too deep to wade where the trail hit the creek. Brenda and Sam sat on the bank and watched Matt carry their packs to the other side using a fallen fir as a bridge. He was crouched high above the water, his arms extended left and right for balance.

Brenda said, "He won't want to stop here. He'll want to make it to our goal. What were those meadows called?"

⬦

At that moment Matt looked back at the two of them and noticed that Brenda's boots were off and her feet were in the creek. As he neared the end of the log, he jumped to the bank. He deposited the final pack and headed across the fir again, watching Brenda and Sam, and realized this would be more than a brief pause on the trail.

What now? Matt thought. For just a moment he had an

impulse to say or do something to express his frustration. His mind lurched in anger at Sam and in pity for himself.

And then a new voice came into it, speaking firmly and with urgency. *If you're really trusting God, why are you so agitated at this change in plans? If you really want to regain her trust, why not just run to her side and show her that you care?*

Matt stopped in shock at this idea. Trusting God? Of course. His thoughts became linear. *Abandon the goal, but abandon it cheerfully. Don't depend on a strategy. Don't depend on anything but God. Don't anticipate anything. Just show her that you love her. And show her now. Trust and love; trust and love. Trust God—and Sam—and love her. Why not?* He stepped off the bridge and hurried to Brenda.

"We'll never make Tunnel Meadows today," Sam said to Brenda as Matt approached. "Look at those blisters, dear. You're in no shape to go another two miles before dark. Besides, there's a lot of up and down between here and there." He turned to Matt. "Thanks for wrangling our packs across the creek. We'll stop here for a break and then help Brenda across downstream. If I remember right, there's a place she can wade. And I know there's a nice flat knoll up out of the draw. I'm bettin' there's a hunters' camp where we can spend the night."

"I don't really care what we do," Brenda said. "For my part, I'd rather be home right now. It doesn't make sense that God would bring us all the way up here to expose Matt's secret life. Why up here with someone we just met?"

Matt stood quietly to her left, head down, staring at the water.

"No offense, Sam," he heard Brenda continue. "But I need my friends and family right now. I never felt more alone in my life than I felt walking over that mountain just now."

"She's right," Matt said, softening his voice. "I can't believe I'm saying this, but I don't care if we reach any of our goals. This is just too hard on her. It seems like a waste to be up here at a time like this." Matt's eyes were wet. "I would be more likely to care about God's will in guiding us toward some meadow in the Sierras if I could understand why God cares about such decisions. But this—this is a life-threatening mistake I've made. We should be making appointments with a counselor rather than thinking about where we're going to sleep in a wilderness tonight."

Brenda looked up at Matt, and he thought he detected a yielding look in her face.

Sam said quietly, "Matt, have a seat." He had pulled his big Bible from his pack before Matt carried it across. He opened it to Ecclesiastes 3. "Let me show you one of the notes I've written in my Bible."

When the couple looked, they saw: *God's signature on events is timing.*

"An old B-17 pilot taught me this when I was in my thirties. I was griping about something that seemed ill-timed in my life, and he held up his hand and said, 'Sam, count on it. God's signature on events is timing.'

"A few years later," Sam went on, "I was studying Ecclesiastes and came across this verse, Ecclesiastes 3:1: 'For everything there is a season, a time for every activity under heaven.'

"Here, let me read the whole section. The Hebrew words for *time* occur in almost thirty places:

> *"For everything there is a season,*
>   *a time for every activity under heaven.*
> *A time to be born and a time to die.*
>   *A time to plant and a time to harvest.*
> *A time to kill and a time to heal.*
>   *A time to tear down and a time to build up.*
> *A time to cry and a time to laugh.*
>   *A time to grieve and a time to dance.*
>   *A time to scatter stones and a time to gather stones.*
>   *A time to embrace and a time to turn away.*
> *A time to search and a time to quit searching.*
>   *A time to keep and a time to throw away.*
> *A time to tear and a time to mend.*
>   *A time to be quiet and a time to speak.*
> *A time to love and a time to hate.*
>   *A time for war and a time for peace."*

Matt looked down at Sam's handwritten notes in the margins, apparently from years ago. Sam began to explain. "Solomon builds his argument around the Hebrew words *zeman* and *'et*, meaning 'appointed time or hour.' Now, those words are used a lot in Hebrew wisdom literature to represent God's appointed time in his plans or intentions."

By this point, yearning to know the bottom line, Matt glanced again at Sam's note at the top of the page. *God's signature on events is timing.* Though he could hardly believe it, his heart was shifting from questioning Sam's reasoning to trusting his wisdom.

❧

As Sam began to expound on his next point, sensing Matt's openness, the young man cut in. "Wait. I have to know something." Matt caught himself and slowed his words. "God's signature. Next to this stream. How would I know? I see Brenda's bloody blister, but I don't know what God would be telling us through this."

"Let me help you by looking at another of Solomon's words in verse 1," Sam replied. "'For everything there is a season, a time for every activity under heaven.'" Sam didn't give Matt a chance to ask the questions he could feel bursting from his heart. "An unusual Hebrew word is translated *activity* or *event* in the last phrase, which says 'an appropriate time for every *activity* on earth' in some versions. This word conveys the idea of delight. Solomon is telling us that there's a delight or a blessing in discerning the timing of God in the activities or events of life. And the more dramatic the event, the more the promise of blessing if we discern God's hand behind it.

"It's ironic," Sam went on. "Most Christians spend 98 percent of their time griping and questioning the timing of the events in their lives. We'll say, 'I don't need this right now,' or attribute the timing of our lives to Satan. 'I'm under attack.' And yet we spend little energy considering what the God of time might be saying to us through the timing of the event. And once again—" Sam stood for emphasis—"the more dramatic the event, the more critical it is to discern the timing as God's."

Sam noticed that Brenda had let a deerfly crawl on her ankle above the waterline for a long time, and when she finally shooed it away, there was no life in her swing. What hope was in her seemed to be washing away into the dark pool of the creek.

He coughed, but his eyes never left Brenda. He knew the pain was trying to burrow into her heart so deep that it would feel safe for years to come, and he fought for her attention. His mind filtered through memories of ways to reach into the black hole of desperate disappointment. Sam stepped into the creek next to her. Water splashed in her face, and he thought he saw her look up out of the corner of her eye. "It would be a shame to miss this God-ordained opportunity," the old pastor said, and he saw Brenda blink involuntarily and look to the other side of the stream.

Brenda mouthed her words into a question that seemed to be in front of her thoughts rather than following them. "God-ordained opportunity?"

"Solomon's main point in the next section is summed up in

verse 11: 'God has made everything beautiful for its own time. He has planted eternity in the human heart, but even so, people cannot see the whole scope of God's work from beginning to end.' God is ultimately responsible for the timing of events in human history. The events of our lives do not randomly happen by chance; God has purposes behind them. Even though we can't know all of his purposes, we know that they're there. We should expect every event in our lives to have meaning. When I preach this, I keep restating the main idea: *Live expectantly; God's signature on events is timing.*"

The late-afternoon breeze blew up the creek, and the leaves whipped around their packs across the way. Wind waves radiated mini breakers, splashing on Brenda's ankles. And the golden trout streaked from under the shadow of the fir to the shelter of the deep undercut banks.

Sam took off his hat and sat on the bank with his White's still in the water. His voice had an edge of urgency. "But this isn't a sermon. This is your life, kids. The timing isn't wrong. It's God's signature on this moment. Don't miss what he's saying to you. It might not feel right to you, but it feels right to God."

"I never thought of that," Brenda admitted, and Sam felt her mind run out in front of her words again, where it belonged. "But if God loves us as much as we say he does, then it certainly makes sense that he would orchestrate the events of our lives to guide us."

"Exactly," Sam said. "I wish I had seen the timing of his

warnings to me about the heavy-handed ways I treated Katie, my daughter."

"Tell me about it." Matt seemed genuinely interested.

"I will," Sam said. "But first, unsling that camera, Brenda. If you'll show me the button to push, I'd like to get a picture of you two sitting on this bank. I think this will be a good reminder to you that God was putting his signature on this event of your life."

He walked a few steps along the bank in his high-top White's and turned to frame the picture in the finder, fumbling for the right button. "This is a fancy camera for an old fireman," he said. "By the way, add *timing* to your list of key words to help you remember how to determine God's will: *trust, relationship, intimacy,* and *timing.* I'll remind you later to write this down. Your verse for this secret to discovering God's will is Ecclesiastes 3:1, and your sentence is: *Live expectantly; God's signature on events is timing.*"

Through the viewfinder he could see the depth of their despondency. Their faces showed the intensity of their spiritual and emotional battle and how they were succumbing to the ugliness of their fears in the midst of all this beauty.

Sam searched for a way to bring them back to the hope of the truth he was teaching, and after he snapped the picture he said, "I remember a dark time in my own life when I missed God's timing." He could feel the shroud of despair lift some as he heard them both take a deep breath.

"When Katie was eleven, I took her on a trip with me. I was speaking at a Bible conference in Chicago, and she suddenly started her period. There we were. I'm trying to prepare for impressive and compelling sermons at the desk in our hotel room, and she's pacing the floor, scared and doubled over with cramping. All I did was gripe at God and her about the timing. 'I can't believe this is happening now,' I protested. She kept telling me she was sorry, and I just let her say it and believe that it was all her fault. My self-centered pride clouded my judgment, and the damage was done. Now I realize it was one of God's greatest opportunities for me to show her that she meant more to me than the ministry."

Sam turned in the creek and looked across the pool, up the slope of the trail toward Tunnel Meadows. "I missed it. It wasn't a test of faith but a gift of timing. Don't miss it, kids." He swore under his breath at the memory. "Sorry. I try not to use that kind of language, but it comes out when I remember times like that. Don't miss it, Matt and Brenda. I may not be a counselor, but I'm here. I know a lot about the Bible and a little about life. And God's put the three of us together on the bank of this creek in this wilderness on this afternoon for one purpose and one purpose only. What do you think that purpose is?"

"He wants us to talk about my sin in the seclusion of this place where no one can hear but you and him." Matt looked across the pool with Sam.

But Sam knew it was not yet resolution Matt wanted; it

was freedom. For months he must have lived in fear, talked to himself in his car, looked with terror at his bride and children, calculated and strategized, and wondered when he would be found out. Now he was ready to give up. Sam hoped that on this day, Matt would stop running and hiding.

Matt sat with his shoulders slumped and spoke. "Brenda?" As Matt waited for her answer, Sam prayed God would give the young man a chance to make things right.

Brenda raised her head and focused her gaze straight forward, her face tightened to fight back tears. Her shoulders shook violently, but she set her jaw and steadied her voice. "Sam, will you help us? I don't know what to do or say next. I don't know if I can forgive Matt, but I know I want to. It's just that I didn't know any of this was going on. And I had no idea that when we decided to come up here with you, I was agreeing to come listen to the most painful news of my life."

Sam picked up a rock and skipped it across the pool, then walked to the bank and stood between Matt and Brenda. He reached down and placed reassuring hands on their shoulders. "You asked for guidance, and God led you to a wilderness. You anticipated insight into your life, and God gave you the truth about your life. The timing of it surprises you, but God's never surprised by timing. It's his signature on events."

Sam knelt and tried to put his arms around the couple, but Matt pulled away uncomfortably. "Don't fear his timing," Sam said, and Brenda melted into his fatherly hug. "Invite it;

embrace it; trust it. I'm thinking there's a great campsite on the other side of this creek, and we'll have the rest of the afternoon and all night if you need to process this."

They sat on the bank as the creek flowed by. The wind died, and a few trout risked rising to feed again on the sunlit surface.

CHAPTER 5
ZIG OR ZAG

Your word is a lamp to guide my feet and a light for my path.

PSALM 119:105

THE HUNTERS' CAMP sat in a flat saddle of deep, decomposed granite on a spur of the ridge separating the trail to Beer Keg Meadow from Long Canyon to the east. Near the center was a sizable fire ring, large enough to hold a late-October warming fire after a cold day of hunting. A shovel stood in the deep ashes, waiting for the next traveler to need its utility. Next to the shovel was a rusty grill, testifying to the same mountain-man code of campsite civility.

Sam studied the layout and then, with the heel of his left boot, furrowed an X in the center of one of the tent sites. He looked down on the X and then took off his hat and put it over his heart. "Father, I pray that this will be a place of mercy and healing and hope tonight. Please be the God of their thoughts and words. In Jesus' name, amen."

He turned and worked his way down to the creek. There was loose shale on the slope, and it became hard to descend and keep his feet. He needed his walking stick and scolded himself for leaving it below. "You got a lot on your mind," he said under his breath, "but pay attention to detail. It's the details that will undo you up here, old fool."

Matt handed Sam his walking stick as he approached. Sam reached for it and instinctively patted the young husband on the back.

"I'm troubled by something, Matt," he said.

"What is that?"

"That you would hide what you know and feel about yourself from me behind the facade of a more impressive you and behind all of that 'I'm-a-commonsense-theology-type-of-Christian' crap."

"Well, I was trying to protect Brenda. I meant to—"

"Stop it," Sam said quickly.

"Stop what?"

"Do you like lying?"

"Of course not."

"You've been lying so long you even forget that you're hiding. You still think that the calm and controlled Matt is what you really look like. If I had an honest-before-God-and-others pill that might heal your marriage and also might destroy it, would you swallow it?"

"What pill?" Matt chuckled nervously and glanced at Brenda, walking toward them along the bank.

"No," said Sam. "You know what I'm going to say, and believe me when I say it might destroy your marriage."

Brenda, now close enough to hear, said, "Sam? What do you mean? Sam?"

Sam could feel the risk of what he was about to do, and he could almost smell Brenda's fear when she stepped toward him. "Sam! Sam!" There was terror in her voice.

But kindness came over him as quickly as the rage toward Matt had, and he said, "There's something else."

✿

Matt's mind defaulted to survival mode and searched frantically, even after this day of painful disclosure, bouncing from one protective scheme to another so the awful depth of his deception might stay hidden. "What are you talking about?" Matt demanded. He looked at Sam with his practiced incredulous face—the one that meant he was a liar, he realized. "Tell me what you're imagining."

The old man's voice softened as he turned to Matt. "Matt, you haven't come clean." Matt closed his eyes. It was launched now, and there was no bringing this one back to earth. "Brenda, if this puts your marriage over the edge, I take the responsibility, and I will tell you I'm sorry for the rest of my days," he barely heard Sam say. "But your husband is still hiding something."

Now the tension that Matt had felt growing in Brenda since morning boiled up to the surface, and her eyes went wide. She turned to Matt, but he couldn't say it wasn't true. "Are you sure, Sam?" she asked.

"I'm sure, young woman of God, and I'm so sorry," Sam said. "Matt, tell her."

Matt tried to compute the options. From the time he'd first stepped over the line with that coworker, he had been thinking of how he could avoid saying what Sam was insisting he say. On his drive back from each secret rendezvous, he'd thought of how Christian and compassionate his care of her and her children really was, and when he had woken up in the middle of the night, he'd puzzled over the alternatives and prepared his defense.

Matt's jaw jutted out under the strain. "I gave her money. Her husband was abusive. Her story is the most hopeless and desperate thing I've ever heard—the worst things a man could do to a woman, he did to her. But it's worse than just that. She was losing her home and would have had to move to Idaho to live with her parents. I was just trying to help. And that's the truth, all of it. Will you still forgive me?"

Brenda looked helplessly at him, for Matt had designed his reasonings to overwhelm. "You gave her money?" She looked to Sam for help.

During Matt's explanation, he'd noticed that Sam had refused to be drawn in. The man continued to gaze at Matt. Brenda watched them both uneasily.

Since Sam remained silent, Matt felt more in control and said, "Yes, I gave her some money because she was needy."

Sam's strength surprised Matt when he grabbed him by the shoulders and shook him. "Dadgummit, Matt, come clean," he shouted. He shook him again and yelled, "I said, come clean! There's more."

Matt's mouth was beginning to form words of defense when Brenda reached for him and slapped him across the face. "How much money are we talking about?" Brenda cried.

The next minute Matt was crawling on his knees like a prize-fighter trying to shake the cobwebs from a knockdown punch. Brenda retreated and he struggled toward her, whimpering. "Thousands, baby. I took the money from bonuses at work I never told you about. And I had set up a bank account you didn't know about. I know; I'm slime. I'm a worthless piece of garbage. I'm sorry. Forgive me. Please forgive me."

Brenda stopped and screamed, "Forgive you? Is that all you have to say? You're a piece of garbage? Of course you are, but if you think it's this easy, think again. I know you, Matt. You just want to feel better, to move on, to stop the pain."

She put her hands on her hips and leaned toward him. "And is that what you think of me, that the money is what I'm upset over? It's just one more way you've deceived me, one more way you've been unfaithful. I could care less about the money. I love you, Matt, and it feels like I'm losing you to this woman."

Matt had felt regret before over the way he'd treated Brenda when his coworker was on his mind. Dismissive. Neglectful. Silent. But now, next to Long Canyon Creek, Matt sat slumped in the decomposed granite and held his face in his hands, drained by the weight of his sin and this wound he had inflicted on his wife's soul. "Brenda," he wailed, "please." He stood and stumbled away from them along the creek. His crying turned to a whimper only when his strength was gone.

*

Sam turned to Brenda, prepared to apologize again. But she cut him off. "Your help feels like hurt right now."

"I don't know any other way to get you through this," Sam said. "Years ago I learned this: when someone's running from their reality or constructing a masked self that is mostly respectable and superficially prosperous and confident, you must surprise them without a warning that you're onto them. Then you must wait for them to look scared, and in that moment, break their knees with the truth. Then, if the sin hasn't turned the lights out in their soul, they will repent. Without the blow to the knees, they will surely die hiding."

"But how did you know Matt was hiding something?" Brenda asked.

"In the same way I know what you're struggling with right now," Sam said. "You're afraid you won't be able to . . ." He paused.

"Forgive him," the young wife said. "Yes. I want to. And then when I think about what he's been doing, I want to tear his eyes out."

"Forgiving him is your only choice." Sam sighed. "The same Spirit that was leading Matt to come clean is leading you now. He's encouraging you to trust what Jesus says about forgiveness, that it's something he wants us to offer and it's the only path to reconciliation. He had to forgive you of your sin before you could have a relationship with him. And you're going to have to forgive Matt. If you don't, your refusal to trust God will get in the way of recognizing God's guidance. I know these are hard words, and I hate piling on such a tough assignment right now. But it's important."

"How do you know these things, Sam?" Brenda repeated. She lowered her eyes. "It's a little creepy, like you're reading our minds."

"You're not the only one asking for guidance up here on this plateau, sweetie." That was Sam's most endearing term for a young woman, and he hoped it made Brenda feel special. "Tonight, if Matt comes right, I'll tell you how God guided me to do what you just saw me do with Matt and to say what I just said to you. I didn't want to, but God said, 'Now!'"

Brenda asked, "Will we make it, Sam?"

"I don't know," Sam admitted. "But now that Matt's taken off his spiritual makeup, there's a good chance. If you can forgive Matt—and you were right not to play into his game of forced forgiveness—and if he's willing to earn your trust . . . you've got a chance. Trust and forgiveness are what God uses to heal. But at least he'll stop hiding and scheming and you won't have to wonder."

"You're an intriguing man," Brenda said.

"No, I'm an old man who has learned to fear the dark places we run to when we hide from God more than the uncertainty of walking toward his soul-piercing light. I've kept my mouth shut too many times when the Lord was telling me to say something hard, and I've lived to regret it. Friends tell me now how they were afraid to break my knees when I was trying to hide from the truth of what I was doing to my daughter. I'd trade a knee-breaking for a heartbreak any day."

Brenda was smiling at him in the dim light of the setting sun. "Like I said, you're an intriguing man."

Sam slipped his hands into the back pockets of his Levi's and took two steps toward Brenda, then leaned back on his right boot. "This moment, standing here next to this creek, isn't about my curious behavior but your faith. You're a courageous woman, Brenda. Your heart is as brave as one of these range cows facing off with a cougar after her calf. You have never, in what I can see in you, run from a fight. But just now something happened that courage can't fix unless it's the courage to believe God."

"I don't know what you mean. Matt's the one whose faith is going to be tested."

"That's not how this works, Brenda. Matt hasn't felt this good since he started sneaking around and taking care of this woman at work. He just unloaded a burden by telling you the truth, and now it's that same truth that the enemy's going to use to try to crush your soul. You don't have the strength to bear it, but God does, and it's your choice."

"I still don't understand."

"Sweetie, your faith paces the healing. You think you're angry with Matt now, just wait until it starts to really hit you. The bitterness will sneak up on you and pounce. You try to tangle with this mountain lion on your own, and you choose to lose. But if you determine to forgive Matt and ask God to give you the courage to believe that you can trust your husband again someday, you've got a chance. It's not much of a chance, but God's great at doing something amazing with small chances."

Sam stared into the trees toward the sound of Matt sobbing and moaning and held his breath. He felt the stalking sadness of sin, the circling of coyotes, the eyes of the cougar. He felt the evil one reaching for Brenda's soul, and he felt helpless to protect her. She was right, of course: his help felt like hurt because it was.

But Sam's mind and his will were set, and his face was unyielding. "This is your chance," he said. "Your husband must repent. He must fight free from the chains of his control and failure, his shame and guilt. But you must forgive. You must fight free from the chains of your bitterness and fear, your anger and anxiety. You must trust God first and me second."

Brenda looked quickly at him and her eyes narrowed. "Easy for you to say, Sam. My husband just admitted to an emotional fling with another woman. Did your wife ever cheat on you?"

Sam shook his head. "I've had to forgive a lot of people for a lot of hurt, but I've never had to forgive what I'm asking you to forgive."

She snapped. "Then you have no idea what this feels like."

Sam avoided letting the conversation take that turn. "It's not me that's telling you to forgive here. It's the Lord Jesus."

Distant crows began to caw, and the air turned cold. The night was coming. The wind of the evening disturbed the water of the pool, and the mini waves collided with the sandy banks. Brenda reached for her pack, dug out her water bottle, and took a drink.

"I wanted to have hope. Like yesterday when you taught us the first principle, Sam—*God doesn't need your strength to guide you, but you do need to trust his strength to recognize his guidance.* It was like God invited me to a canvas and asked me to draw. And when I took my pencil, a sketch began, romantic and elegant. I had hope that my life, which feels confusing and aimless at times, could become wonderfully meaningful—if I could learn to trust in God's will for my marriage, my family, and me. But now the scene's turned from fantasy and romance to nightmarish reality. Since Matt's confession, my sketch has a new theme, like a Shakespearean tragedy, with all of its hopeless twists and turns."

Sam held his bottom lip steady, and tears rimmed his eyes. "That was your first mistake. *You* took your pencil and the sketch began. God just took the pencil from your hand.

"God doesn't need your strength to guide you. He doesn't need you to tell him what the sketch of your life should be. But you really do need to trust his strength to recognize his guidance, Brenda. It's liberating. He and I love you too much to let you have your own way."

❧

Sam's gentle words broke up Brenda's carefully crafted defense, which she had intended to begin: *For all these years I have loved Matt with my whole heart, and now I can't believe that you're asking me to just forgive—*

"No," she heard herself say instead. Sam's words echoed in her mind. *He and I love you. . . . I love you . . . love . . . you . . . love . . . you . . . God loves you. . . . I love you.* She turned away. She took deep breaths. Her heart throbbed. She spun around and moved toward Sam, then pounded her fists on his chest.

"No!" Brenda repeated. "I can't! Don't ask me to!" She struck the old man's chest until she was afraid she would hurt him. "I can't!" she said again and again until what she was really feeling—the feeling that she didn't want to admit because she knew it would break her—finally formed into a sentence from her lips.

"I want to be loved." She buried her head in Sam's chest and cried like she hadn't cried since she was a little girl.

Sam held her and stroked her hair. "I know, sweetie. I know."

He helped her to a granite rock and handed her his handkerchief as she stared toward the creek and began speaking again. "If God loves me, if you love me . . . then I should trust him . . . and you."

"We all need to trust him right now." Sam spoke softly in case Matt was close enough to hear. "Trust will give us the courage to keep going. You trusted me enough to summon the courage to walk over that ridge on blistered feet. And God will give you the courage to walk through this mess with Matt, if you'll trust the Lord enough to do what he says. Forgive Matt. Your husband has a good heart." Sam paused. "He doesn't think so right now, but he does. Don't get me wrong. What he did was stupid, sinful, and self-serving, and there's no excuse for it. Still, I believe that he's finally come clean, with you and God."

Brenda looked up. She was strangely calm and confident. "Teach me the words again, Sam."

"Trust."

"God doesn't need my strength to guide me, but I do need to trust his strength to recognize his guidance," Brenda said.

"Relationship."

"Make sure I'm all in for Jesus."

"That's right, sweetie. Then, *intimacy*."

"Stay within the circle of intimacy with God, and trust him that you're on the dot. Am I on the dot, Sam?"

"If you're forgiving Matt, you're on the dot. That's his revealed will for every believer. Next word: *timing*."

"I want to forgive him, Sam. I really do. I want to. I can't remember that last sentence about timing."

"Live expectantly; God's signature on events is timing."

Brenda drew a breath and stared blankly, and her voice lowered to a whisper. "If you would have told me a few days ago that when my husband confessed to an emotional affair that included giving thousands of dollars to some woman at work, I would feel closer to God, I would have said you were crazy. But that's how I feel right now. It's like in spite of all this pain in my heart, I have more confidence that Matt and I are on the dot of his will, as you call it, than at any other time in our lives."

"You've forgiven him, haven't you?" Sam smiled.

"Yes."

"*Trust, relationship, intimacy,* and *timing,*" Sam said. "Those are your four words, and we'll add another one tonight. Here, let me doctor that foot for you, and then we'll wrangle this gear up to our camp. I'll come back for Matt when he's done."

"Crying?" Brenda asked.

"Repenting."

The two of them worked the gear to the hunters' camp and set up the tents. The young couple's tent went on the pad marked with an X. As they hiked up and down the hill, the sound of Matt's moaning faded, and all was quiet where the Tunnel Meadows trail crossed Long Canyon Creek.

✦

Matt walked into camp after supper, sat on the ground, and leaned back against a log next to the fire. His mind was a fog and his stomach held a sediment of pain. He tried to focus his eyes on the two faces in the glow of the flames, but it was impossible. The levees of his mathematical mind had failed to protect him from the tsunami of thoughts and emotions. The walls were down, and waves of uncomfortable feelings washed over his soul, drowning him. After some time he came to the surface just long enough to gasp for air and take in words and sentence fragments before sinking again into the murkiness. In between desperate trips to the surface, Matt pieced together the timeline that had ended in the exact way he had dedicated himself to avoiding.

First Matt had let his guard down and tried to help his coworker. He remembered that first time he had felt sorry for her at the business luncheon. It had seemed so harmless; she was just a friend who needed to talk. So he'd suppressed the warning in his stomach—a misgiving he now admitted was the Spirit at work.

His mind pictured the drive to Newport and the walk around Balboa Island. He thought of her weeping and how good it had felt to speak wisdom into her life that gave her hope. But he had also felt something coming from her that he knew he couldn't trust. That was when God was telling him to stop it all and confess to Brenda.

He thought of how his coworker kept needing more of him. He'd felt responsible for her, but also guilty over all the lies he was having to tell. It was agonizing to keep all of those lies straight. He wondered why he hadn't gone to someone for advice and counsel. How could he have been so stupid?

Finally, he recalled the smile on the woman's face, her appreciation when he'd first given her some money, and how powerful it had made him feel—until he came home that day and the transmission went out on the van and they had to put the repair on the charge card. It hadn't felt good to be some other family's hero then. The next time she'd asked for money and he'd said yes, he knew he was in too deep.

The acidic question Matt had once asked God—*How do I tell Brenda?*—was now answered, but a more haunting question slipped into his heart: *Will she forgive me?*

The conversation around the fire slowly pulled Matt back to the here and now, and he couldn't suppress his skepticism as he thought about the old man's teaching of the circle and the dot. "If this is a dot, it's not ours. Our dot was supposed to be in some meadow with a tunnel in it," he said to no one. "I may not be a mountain man, but I know enough to see that this isn't a meadow. We're not there yet."

Sam's voice was soft and his face kind. "Careful, son. You're wrung out because your recent behavior didn't square with your heart. That kind of fracture makes a man skeptical, just like Thomas. They call him Doubting Thomas, but if you read the story carefully, he was courageous. I think he just couldn't accept the fact that he had run when the Savior needed him. Like you, he was wrung out, and it boiled over into cynicism.

"You want to know how this can be the dot of God's will," the old man said. "I was just explaining this to Brenda." He stood and began to pace slowly around the fire, staying out of the smoke.

"Brenda, read the verse I had you turn to—Psalm 119:105."

Brenda looked beautiful in the glow of the fire. She fixed her headlamp beam on her Bible. "'Your word is a lamp to guide my feet and a light for my path.'"

Sam stopped to pour a cup of hot coffee and handed it to Matt. "Two interesting Hebrew words used there. The *lamp* refers to a small bowl of oil with a floating wick that people kept by their beds. It could guide their next step reliably, but it was limited to protecting them from stumbling over something in the dark. The *light* was a torch that kept them on the path, but it, too, was limited.

"Context is paramount here," Sam said. "Psalm 119 is the longest chapter in the Bible, and I believe it's a collection of prayers and thoughts about the wonder of God's Word. We don't know who the final editor was, but I suspect it was Ezra suffering under the challenges of trying to reestablish God's people in the Promised Land." Sam had shifted into Bible-teacher mode. "Like I was saying, whoever it was found refuge and strength by meditating on the Word of God. Ezra, or the writer, divided the psalm into eight-verse sections, each beginning with the next letter of the Hebrew alphabet. So it was like *A* is for this wonder of the Scriptures and *B* is for that one."

Matt was intrigued in spite of himself, but then Sam got

back to his point. "Anyway, verses 105 to 112 all begin with the Hebrew letter *nun* or *N*, and they explain how God's Word guides us. Okay, Brenda, read that entire section."

Brenda concentrated her light on the page.

Your word is a lamp to guide my feet
*   and a light for my path.*
I've promised it once, and I'll promise it again:
*   I will obey your righteous regulations.*
I have suffered much, O LORD;
*   restore my life again as you promised.*
LORD, accept my offering of praise,
*   and teach me your regulations.*
My life constantly hangs in the balance,
*   but I will not stop obeying your instructions.*
The wicked have set their traps for me,
*   but I will not turn from your commandments.*
Your laws are my treasure;
*   they are my heart's delight.*
I am determined to keep your decrees
*   to the very end.*

"The psalmist commits to obeying God's Word because he trusts it to guide him," Sam said. "The Word of God is a guiding light, but it's a lamp and a torch rather than a floodlight or a crystal ball.

"It's sad," the old pastor went on. "Many sincere Christians conclude that the Bible doesn't offer specific guidance because they've been taught to think in terms of the crystal ball or floodlight view. Someone has told them to claim verses in a hocus-pocus, if-you-have-enough-faith-God-has-to-do-it way. Or they've demanded that God give them a verse that will flood his light beyond their immediate path to the rest of their lives so they can avoid all pain and make no mistakes. Of course they're deeply disappointed and consequently stop reading their Bibles expectantly when it comes to seeking his will."

Sam bent down to pour himself some coffee. "You still good, Brenda? Need a warm-up?" Brenda shook her head no. "How about you, Matt?"

Matt had not moved. He followed the pot desperately with his eyes, and Sam refilled his cup. "A few steps at a time," Matt said. "Is that what you're saying?"

"Yes, but it's not only a few steps at a time; it's where the path you're following lies." He put the pot down and began to pace slowly.

"Let me tell you about the first picture that comes to my mind when I read those words about God's Word being a lamp to my feet and a torch to light my path. It was in '70, or was it '71? Yeah, '70, that's right. Anyway, one night my crew had fought fire all the way to the top of the north slope of the mouth of the Kern River. You probably passed the mouth of the Kern in the dark on your way up here, so you can't appreciate how steep that country is. Well, we got to the top, and the only thing to do was go back down the other side in the middle of the night. There was no moon that night, so all we had were our headlamps. And you can bet they didn't work as nice as those REI units you're wearing. By the way, you mind turning those things off? You're blinding me every time you look up to listen."

It was dark in the flicker of the evening's fire. Old Sam, who Matt suspected was still young enough in his mind to fight a fire in the Kern Canyon, described the Mouth Fire of 1970 so that Matt felt as if he were there with the fire crew.

"She's a steep one, that canyon. Wild oats up to your elbows and straight down. A professional forester, name of Schuster, who was a good hand every fireman trusted, led us down that canyon wall. I was the lead shovel, and all night long he was tellin' me, 'Sam, walk to my light.' So I'd take the line the next ten or twenty yards to his light. 'Wait here in the dark,' he'd tell me. 'Don't move an inch.' An' I'd stop the crew with them griping about having to spend so much time standing still in the dark and all. Then old Schuster would look up at me from the next location and we'd do her again."

Sam went on. "I have to admit that I wondered if Schuster knew what he was doing. It felt like we were zigzagging all over that canyon and takin' the longest possible route to the bottom."

He stepped toward them and crouched like he was about to

begin a war dance. Matt and Brenda looked at each other and chuckled. Sam was seemingly too into his story to notice.

"We hooked her early morning. Sorry, kids. *Hooked* is fire talk for surrounding the fire with a fire line—what firefighters construct around the fire to contain it. The basic idea is to separate the fire from the fuel—you know, grass, brush, trees. Am I getting too technical? Anyway, this was a grass fire, so our line was about a three-foot-wide strip, scraped down to bare dirt." He didn't wait for them to answer and got lost in the story again. "Schuster gathered us out on a couple of big rocks on the north bank of the Kern and said, 'Look up, boys!'"

Sam gazed toward the heavens as if he could see it in his mind.

"We were slapping each other on the back and talking about what we were going to have for breakfast after our great victory, the way young men will. The next minute there was a hush that swallowed up the roar of the Kern."

Sam stepped up to the fire and swept his coffee cup across the sky, showering the coals with coffee. "Joe, a big kid from the Tule Reservation, jumped to a rock in the middle, turned, and said for all of us, 'Good Lord!'"

He smiled wryly. He knelt down beside the couple. "All night long we were building our fire line on the edge of a cliff that fell straight into the river hundreds of feet below. Old Schuster wasn't only guiding us a step and twenty yards at a time. He was protecting us from a danger we didn't know was there."

Sam's voice deepened. "Good Lord, indeed. Don't tell me that your Father hasn't brought you to this dot, right to the edge of the darkness, in twenty-yard portions. His Word moved you to seek his will. His Spirit moved you to risk meeting me up in this wilderness. He has been shining his light twenty yards down the path and to the edge of the darkness to bring you here. This is your dot. It's not Tunnel Meadows; it's here—Matt and Brenda, sitting around this campfire, on this spur, on this night, after Matt wore himself out repenting from a sin he'd tried to hide."

The old man looked Matt in the eye. "She's going to forgive you, Matt. And maybe, just maybe, you'll earn her trust again and you two can get on with your life."

Sam stood and took a deep breath. "You've got the rest of the night to talk and pray about this. But don't forget to thank the Lord for the cliffs he's guided you along during the last two days. God's not just showing you the way he wants you to go. He's protecting you from things you can't know."

Matt looked at Sam without speaking, mulling this over in his mind.

"I've been talking for a long time," Sam said. "Brenda, grab your sketchbook and write this down. Matt, get out your journal. This lesson on finding God's will is coming to a close."

Matt wasn't sure where his journal was, but he focused attentively on Sam.

"Now you know the fifth word, the verse, and the sentence.

The word is *protection*, the verse is Psalm 119:105, and the sentence is, *God's will is a flashlight, not a crystal ball; walk to the edge of the darkness and wait.*"

And the dramatic truth his firefighting story illustrated seemed to satisfy Sam. He set his cup on a log and walked toward his tent. "I'm turning in, kids. This day ended with hope."

Matt shook his head in the dark, shook it hard in a dawning. *If God loves me, then he protects me. He guides me by his Word and shows me the path to walk. A safe path, because he knows where the danger lies. So I walk to the edge of the darkness and wait.* He was waking up to a lot more than the sounds of the night. Matt felt he had to say something—something God was telling him to say.

His next few yards were suddenly obvious. Brenda loved him. She had told him that plainly and now she was living it, and he was a fool not to trust her and God to forgive him for his involvement with this other woman. He turned to the bride of his youth and said softly, "I'm so sorry, Brenda. Will you really? Forgive me?"

She smiled a little, enough to give him hope.

Matt realized he was hungry. Brenda spoke with a tenderness in her voice that was new to this evening. "I saved you some of the stew Sam cooked for dinner. I love you, Matt."

Matt noticed that she had pulled his journal from his pack and set it next to him. He opened it and wrote, *God's will is a flashlight, not a crystal ball. Psalm 119:105. I'm on the dot.*

The fire had gone out, and Matt and Brenda sat in the dim glow of the coals. Their quiet conversation lasted late into the star-filled night. The Big Dipper circled the North Star above, and an owl screeched, hunting the banks of Long Canyon Creek below. From the east, toward Olancha Peak, came the sound of thunder.

CHAPTER 6

DOUBT OR CERTAINTY

Send me a sign of your favor.

PSALM 86:17

BRENDA ROLLED OVER against Matt for warmth. In the deepest places of her heart, the hope from last night's conversation with Matt under the stars collided with the fear of her anxious thoughts. She hadn't yet processed the highs and lows of the last couple of days in this wilderness. Brenda was especially afraid of trusting happiness and hope, having been so recently disappointed. But she wanted to face this dawn with the warmth of last night's intimacy.

She squinted in the dark, trying to wring images of Matt's betrayal from her head. And she tried to erase the picture of Matt and that other woman walking on the beach. Her body shivered and her mind tried to suppress the cold reality of what she never imagined would be true of her. *I trusted him before, and he was carrying on with another woman. How do I know he won't deceive me again, that he isn't lying still?* Anxious thoughts came quickly, so it didn't take long for her to silently cry out to God in prayer. *But if this is my only choice—to trust Matt again—I need you to do something to let me know it's what you want, that you're with me in this.* When she finished her prayer, she became aware of another voice in the dark.

◢

Outside the tent Sam knelt in the dirt, gently blowing on warm embers to encourage the morning fire. The old man looked hopelessly at the struggling flame, and gradually his sorrow and ache grew into words.

"You took her before we were through," he said helplessly. "Nobody did this but you. Now I'm all by myself. Everybody knew she was the heart of our family. My sweet Annie. She was the good one, the one people went to when they needed more than my words." He paused, and his voice broke. "If only I could be up here with Annie and Katie and build this fire for them. I could cook breakfast for the two of them and make tea with two sugars and a dusting of creamer just the way my Annie loved it. And we could talk about Katie's life, because she always trusted her mother's love more than mine. And who would blame her? I trusted Annie's love more than any other. We'd sit next to this fire and pray for our little girl together."

Sam took a breath, then continued in a rhythm of well-worn

sentences. He repeated old words from a lifetime of prayer: "'But you, O Lord, are a God of compassion and mercy, slow to get angry and filled with unfailing love and faithfulness. Look down and have mercy on me. Give your strength to your servant; save me. Send me a sign of your favor.' And . . . if you would, please, kind Sir . . ."

Sam's eyes were blinded with tears, and he turned his face to heaven with arms reaching for his God. "And please, if I'm on the right path in this battle for my Katie's soul—if I'm thinking straight here about leaving her alone until she comes to her senses, until she sees that I was right to stand in her way—if this is your will, give me a sign of encouragement. Please, my Father, just like you've done so many times. I need it now. A sign of encouragement." He stood and walked weakly toward his gear, wiping tears from his whiskered face with his right sleeve. "In Jesus' name, amen."

🌿

Brenda was suddenly aware of Matt turning toward her. "You okay?" he asked, half-awake.

"I'm fine," she said. "Just got a little chill. Go back to sleep."

Brenda hoped Sam hadn't heard them. She closed her eyes, and her mind saw and felt this chapter of the old man's story. She pictured him on his knees outside her tent. *This isn't theory for him,* she thought. *He's living it.*

Her thoughts were intense and on the edge of shame.

I wondered why he hardly mentioned his wife. He's alone, but we're so preoccupied with our own mess, we never asked.

Brenda opened her eyes for a moment. She was connecting the pain in Sam's heart to his desperate request for something. What was it he asked for? A sign of encouragement? She wondered how she could ask him what he meant without admitting that she had eavesdropped on his intimate conversation with God, but before she'd figured it out, she drifted back to sleep.

It was late in the morning when they woke again, and Brenda felt just a little embarrassed. As she and Matt crawled from their tent, they tried to demonstrate their proficiency at packing up, but Sam must have noticed their hurried pace. He looked at his watch and asked, "What's your rush?"

Brenda realized that the mountain man had not yet begun to "strike camp," as he'd said yesterday morning as a signal for them to pack for the day's journey. They didn't finish their relaxed breakfast of oatmeal and bacon until eleven, and Sam poured them each another cup of coffee.

He returned the pot to the fire, pulled his map from his back pocket, then knelt between Matt and Brenda. "I knew you were worn out last night," he said. "We'll take her easy today and just work our way back to Casa by way of the Big Dry. Easy walk, mostly downhill, and it'll give you two a chance to learn how to read a map." Then he spread the map on the ground and coughed nervously. "I mean, you may want to come up here on your own someday without an old man slowing you down." He sniffed, and his voice broke. "If you decide you like this country and it lodges in your heart like it has mine."

Brenda wanted to follow up with a question, but she decided against it.

Although there were blue skies over the plateau, storm cloud tops were beginning to build in the east. Through the ponderosa and fir came the thuds of thunder and the occasional gunshot bangs of lightning strikes.

Matt and Brenda looked intently at Sam. He reached over the map and ground some tinder-dry pine needles in his hand. "Storms rarely kick up this time of year. It's still a ways off and we're good. Just hope there's some rain with it when it comes through. Dry lightning's not a good thing up here this late in the summer."

"Does that mean there's danger of a fire?" asked Matt. "It was about a year ago that some backpackers were overrun by a fire in the San Gabriels. It was all over the news in SoCal."

"These aren't the San Gabriels," Sam said. "That's some of the steepest country in the west. This storm might kick up a fire, maybe, but it will more than likely have some moisture with it. Besides, those backpackers didn't have me with them."

He smiled and pointed to the map. "We're right here on this little green area with no contour lines, just west of Long Canyon. See that? Right there's the creek, that blue line."

Brenda forgot the thunder and studied the map. Sam's scarred finger traced the route. "Okay, you two." He looked up, and Brenda noticed he hadn't called them "kids." She smiled at him. "We'll cross back over the creek and head south down that trail that looks like a series of red dashes. All you have to do is follow the trail as it turns east, and about a mile out you'll break from the trees into that big patch of white on the map. That's Big Dry Meadows. Once you're there it's a piece of cake. Just follow the meadows south, stay on the trail over that little peak, and you're back in Casa. Shouldn't take more than a couple of hours."

ø

Matt was grateful for the three bowls of oatmeal he'd eaten; the long and agonizing day of repentance had wrung his soul. He knew he must have help and healing. And what better place to receive it than up here, with Sam and Brenda? He looked down the hill at the place of his full confession and shuddered. Then his soul began to relax within him for the first time in recent memory.

The sun was high in the afternoon sky by the time they worked their way over the creek, and the east wind scattered pine needles across the trail to Big Dry Meadows. Brenda walked ahead, and she held the map folded as Sam had taught her.

Eventually Brenda slowed and stopped where the trail entered the trees. Matt could see her confidence diminish, her courage disappear. He joined her and leaned into the map. The couple circled left, Brenda holding the map at arm's length. "We must be missing something," Matt said.

For suddenly what had seemed so clear on the map was anything but clear on the ground. There on the south side of Long Canyon Creek one trail became four, and it was impossible to distinguish which choice represented the broken red lines on the map.

From behind them came old Sam's voice. "Brenda," he called, "you having some trouble? I'll be right there." Matt turned to see Sam quicken his gait and pull alongside them. "Oh, I see. You have to understand that the bear, deer, and cattle can't read a map. They just get where they're going, and sometimes they're not going where you want to go. That's why you'll see so many options at a choke point like what we have here. This is when you have to find a blaze and trust your map."

"A blaze?" Matt snapped, his old impatience getting the best of him. "How were we supposed to know that?"

"Patience, young Matt. One lesson at a time. There's a lot to learn. The trails of the high country are marked by blazes— hatchet chops in the bark of trees up high above the level of winter snow." Sam raised his arm and pointed down the trail. "There's your next blaze. See it there to the left on that old fir? That blaze tells you where the path on the map lies. Kind of like 'walk to the edge of the darkness and wait,' except it's 'walk to the next blaze and wait.' Always be careful to stop and find your next blaze when there're multiple options, or you're going to head down the wrong path not knowing where you left the trail."

"Kind of like life," Matt said quietly.

Brenda expanded on his observation. "Just like life—move from sign to sign."

Matt sighed. He knew she felt like she needed to make that point for his benefit, since he usually discounted such mystical views.

"I'm heading for that blaze," Brenda said. "This is easy. Just move from blaze to blaze. I'm on my way to Big Dry Meadows, men, even if I have to go by myself."

Sam turned to Matt. "Sounds like an invitation to me. After you, young man." Matt moved into the trees.

"There's another blaze!" Brenda pointed excitedly to a mark at the top of a saddle in the ridge.

Matt wasn't convinced. "It looks different from the last one."

"You just don't trust the signs," Brenda said playfully. "It's a blaze for sure."

◢

Sam waited a moment before the trees and looked east. "Storm'll be here tomorrow," he said under his breath.

He walked after Matt and Brenda, following at a distance. When the couple moved quickly down the other side of the ridge, Sam stopped at the top and watched them veer right off the trail into the wilderness. "Poor greenhorns," he said. "They forgot everything I just told them, mistook a gouge in that pine for a blaze, and followed that old cow trail into nowhere."

The path on the ground grew fainter as Sam continued to follow his companions into the woods. The manzanita was crowding in gradually, and in the shadows of the pine and fir, the young couple slowed their pace and scanned the trees for the next blaze.

Matt appeared to see a break in the trees and ran ahead. "Here's the meadow."

Be patient, old man, Sam told himself. He remembered his own greenhorn years and the difficulty of learning to read a map, navigate, and reach an objective in the wilderness. Not only was the whole endeavor complicated, but it all occurred in an alien environment.

"Here we are. Big Dry Meadows!" Matt called, falsely assured. "Why do they call this little piece of the wilderness big?" he wondered with raw wrongheadedness.

Brenda stepped into the tiny meadow with the map in her left hand. "This can't be right. Big Dry Meadows is long, and there's a creek running along the left side. We're lost, Matt!"

Sam came confidently to the meadow's edge. He saw the confusion on their faces and felt his opportunity. He could lecture them for their failure to look for clear blaze signs marking the trail. But Brenda and Matt here, looking helplessly at him, were ready for an even greater lesson. Sam suddenly felt a deep love for this husband and wife, and he knew God was urging him to introduce them to signs of encouragement. He put his arm around Brenda.

Brenda handed Sam the map. He motioned Matt to his side so they could study the map together.

"Do you know where we left the trail?" Matt asked.

Brenda said, "I was following Matt, and the next thing I know we're standing here in the wrong place with no idea of how we got here."

"I don't know why you have to blame me, Brenda. You're the one who misread the signs."

"Well, you were the one running through the forest saying, 'Follow me.'"

The young couple was clearly embarrassed. They'd ignored Sam's advice once again. As Matt studied the map, he said without lifting his head, "Sam, it's difficult to learn everything there is about finding our way in a wilderness in just a few days. Can you take us back to the last trail blaze so we can make our way to the right meadow?"

"Sure. But let's try something new. It's called dead reckoning."

"Dead reckoning?" Brenda responded. "That seems ominous."

"It can be," Sam said. "But it's a necessary skill, because no matter how well the path is marked, there are times when you just have to trust the map and find your way without a trail."

"I'd like that," Matt said.

"We'll start simple," Sam said. "You see this little meadow, this white space on the map? That's where we are. Just walk southwest to the other end, and that puts us there." He pointed. "When we hit the trees—the green part on the map—it gets more complicated. We have to be careful not to veer left or right, but to stay southwest. I've got a compass, so that helps. What we're looking for is this next meadow. See it? It's not named, but Lost Trout Creek runs through it."

"How long do you think it will take us?" Brenda asked.

Sam laughed. "Sounds like you're ready for some dead reckoning. Maybe an hour and we'll be there. It's a nice meadow, kind of a special place because only cowboys and Forest Service types ever visit." He leaned back from the map and looked at them. "But here's the deal. You two are going to have to find it on your own."

On their hike through the green part of the map, Brenda noticed things she had not seen before. She felt the steeper slope to their left and saw the cow tracks in the decomposed granite, moving down the easy descending path as they walked. When they finally came into the meadow, Matt expressed a confidence so new that Brenda couldn't help noticing. And then Matt began saying to her, in rhythm with his breathing, "Dead reckoning, dead reckoning. We did it. Dead reckoning. Finding our way without sign one!"

Suddenly Sam appeared out of the trees, and he passed by the couple as confidently as a mountain goat moved. "Oh, it's a sign, all right. You bet. Stumbling into this little gem of a meadow is a sign from God. Follow me across Lost Trout Creek and we'll make camp." He pulled his cap down low over his eyes. "Matt, you're about to catch some of the nicest golden trout on the plateau. Brenda, get out your sketchbook. You think you've just seen some nice country? This is one of the sweetest little corners of God's creation." He turned his head and looked at the unspoiled meadow. "I forgot about this place, but God didn't. He brought us here, kids, to what we'll call Lost Trout Meadow. And it's a sign. A sign of encouragement."

Because Brenda assumed Sam embraced her definition of a sign from God, she began speaking of encounters and visions she'd had: how the light shining on a painting in a doctor's office looked like a cross, so she knew that was God's doctor for her; how a dream about a fire in her kitchen always reminded her to check the stove before she left the house; how she sometimes saw Jesus' face in a cloud, which always assured her that God was with her.

Sam was quiet for so long that it made Brenda uncomfortable. She was relieved when he spoke again. But the old man's pitch lowered. There was a schooling in it.

"Brenda, there's a difference between a sign of encouragement we ask and wait for and what you're talking about. I'm not saying that God can't guide in mysterious ways, but there's a fine line between a sign from God and superstition."

Matt leaned in to speak, but Sam stopped him with a glance.

"Brenda," Sam said, "I've thought about this for a great many hours, and I still don't know how to fully explain the difference. God's will is a mystery, but his guidance is beyond superstition. It's his hand on our lives in ways that his Spirit makes clear. I'm not saying you're wrong in what you think he's saying to you; I'm just saying be careful."

Brenda struggled for the rest of the afternoon with this recalibration of the definition of a sign and her guilt over having eavesdropped on Sam's desperate prayer for his daughter that morning. The busyness of making camp and watching Sam and Matt catch some fish frustrated every opportunity to ask the pastor what he meant by a sign of encouragement.

As Sam prepared the afternoon's catch for dinner, Brenda looked over the campfire to the orange of the sunset on the ridges as dusk came into the meadow. A big buck emerged from the trees, looked their way, and bent to graze.

"You see that?" Matt whispered next to her. "He just looked at us and went on. Amazing. Like we're not even here. Get a picture, Bren."

Brenda reached for her camera and brought it to her face. When the buck looked up again, she snapped the shutter. The click spooked him, and he was gone.

Sam walked to the fire and placed five fat trout on the grill. The fish sizzled over the coals. "*There's* a sign of encouragement if ever I saw one," Sam said. "Golden trout on the fire and a big old mulie buck wandering into camp and smiling at us. God's been good to me today. I asked him for this sign, and he sent it."

Matt found his notebook and pen and said, "Sign of encouragement?" Brenda wasn't surprised by his skepticism.

Then Sam laughed and gave Matt a pleased nod. "I wondered when one of you was going to take the bait." He smiled and turned the fish on the grill. "That's the next principle of finding God's will: *Ask for a sign of encouragement.*"

Brenda watched him from across the fire. With a smile that was becoming her special look for Sam, she said, "I like my fish well done too."

"But wait," Matt said with a concentration that didn't resemble his intensity before he'd repented. "Let's get back to this sign of encouragement. I thought we were dead reckoning and that meant there weren't any signs."

"Well done it is, Brenda." Sam picked up his Bible and turned to the Psalms. "Here we are, Psalm 86. This is where I turn when I need reassurance. Like I did this morning. I'm trying desperately to repair my relationship with my daughter, and I just needed to know that I was on the right path. Not literally, because I don't get lost up here. But in life, amid its disappointments and heartaches."

Brenda stared down at her camera and tried to hold her face expressionless. She wondered if Sam knew she had listened to his morning prayer for a sign of encouragement.

Sam looked up from his Bible. "The raw honesty of David's

words initially attracted me to his prayer." He glanced down again to read. "He says in the first two verses, 'Bend down, O Lord, and hear my prayer; answer me, for I need your help. Protect me, for I am devoted to you. Save me, for I serve you and trust you. You are my God.'"

Sam checked the fish on the grill. "I like that. David felt like I was feeling this morning. I'm trying to do what I can to reach Katie. But I have doubts and feel lost sometimes. Like you two this afternoon when you wandered off the trail. Like we all feel when we're dead reckoning, in the high country or through life. 'Okay, Lord. I'm trying here. You better answer me because I'm trusting in you.'"

He turned toward Brenda, who met his gaze reluctantly. "I think that's a particular way to discern between superstition and a sign," Sam said. "If we're asking for and expecting God to encourage us in a specific mess, heartache, or decision in life, he often responds with a sign."

Brenda's fear diminished. Sam was just telling his story. "Oh!" she said, relieved. The other two turned and looked at her, and she tried to deflect them. "This is great, Sam." She nodded for him to go on. "A sign of encouragement. Tell us more."

"This psalm is so familiar to me." Sam studied his Bible again. "David asks for God's merciful deliverance in verses 3 through 10 and then for his guidance in verse 11." Sam read aloud. "'Teach me your ways, O Lord, that I may live according to your truth!' And then, amazingly, in verse 17 he wants God to verify that he is granting David's requests with solid evidence. 'Send me a sign of your favor.'

"The Hebrew word David uses means a sign for good, an indicator that God is kindly disposed toward him." He turned his Bible facedown on a rock, passed Matt and Brenda their plates, and pointed to the trout. "When you think they're done enough for you, grab one. The beans are ready. Let's eat."

They sat by the fire with their plates in their laps as Sam continued. "David was asking for a sign that would motivate him to stay the course he was already on, a miraculous intervention to assure him he was on the right path. The best way I know to describe that kind of sign is with the word *encouragement*."

Matt stopped chewing and swallowed. "So, like Gideon, Christians can ask God for a sign before they make a decision?"

"That's not exactly what I'm talking about. Gideon was asking for signs before he moved forward. This is more like the story of Daniel. He took great risks by obeying God instead of the king of Babylon. He trusted God and moved forward in faith. And God affirmed his obedience and direction in life with numerous signs and miracles. What I'm saying is to ask God for a sign of encouragement after you've launched out in faith. And then expect it! The sign of encouragement, I mean. You're not telling him what the sign has to be like Gideon did. You just need to recognize it when it comes. It's not a demand; it's a request. And when it comes, it's not a directive as much as a confirmation."

Sam went on. "Dead reckoning through life requires careful courage, like you two had when you were making your way to this place. You were careful in your steps, pausing to recheck the map and look at the landscape. But you kept going in spite of your fears and insecurities."

"It's a balance," the old pastor said. "The map never lies and neither does the Bible, so we have to carefully study the truth before taking our next step. But we still have to take that step."

"I never thought of it that way," Matt admitted. "But if we're carefully taking these steps, then it's okay to ask God to strengthen our courage with one of these signs of encouragement?"

Brenda was wondering about that too.

"Exactly," Sam said. "I wish I had known this truth as a young believer when I first tried to discern God's will."

"What do you mean?" Brenda asked.

Sam's voice became deeper. "Well, in most decisions I faced, I didn't know if I was reading the map correctly or not. I was just dead reckoning through life, wondering if I was missing something God wanted me to see. If you asked me whether I was on the right path, I would say either 'I don't know' or 'I think so.' If you asked why I thought so, I would answer, 'I haven't fallen off a cliff lately' or 'It doesn't seem that God is upset with me.' It was almost as if my main objective was to minimize the damage."

Brenda was engrossed. "That's it—that's it. Now tell us how to live another way."

The mountain man stopped talking and glanced in the

direction of Brenda's interruption. She looked back, embarrassed. "Sorry."

"Don't apologize," Sam said. "You're anticipating where this is all leading." He paused for emphasis, then repeated her words. "How to live another way. Well, with us, devoted followers of Christ, it's not just minimizing the damage of our decisions," he explained. "We have a God who cares and who shows up, but on his own terms. We don't have to stumble through life wondering if we're on the right path. If those who push him out of their lives want to make their own way, let 'em. But not us."

The embarrassment left Brenda. "But not us! And why? Because . . . because we have a God who will give us a sign, a sign of encouragement. That's why!" She remembered her despairing cry to God that morning, asking him to assure her that she should risk trusting Matt again. "Go on, Sam. Tell us more."

"You got it, sweetie. You can explain it yourself."

"No, you. I'm just grasping this. Tell us how it works."

"Sure," Sam said. "When we're dead reckoning through life and we're wondering if we're on the right path and our heart begins to doubt—"

"We ask God for a sign of encouragement," Brenda cried. "And he guides us to a meadow no one would ever find and brings a big buck into camp and we catch the best-tasting trout in the universe just so we can know that he's watching and he's saying we're on the right path. Tell us about that, Sam."

"Well," said Sam, "I've been teaching and living Psalm 86 for over thirty years. And when someone who loves the Lord Jesus is trying to follow him with the courageous faith of a dead-reckoning Christian, I've seen him show up in dramatic fashion." He cut into the twelve-inch trout on his plate. "This is a nice 'un, Matt. I think we've pretty much covered it, kids." He scooped up some beans, came to the other side of the fire, and sat down next to Brenda.

"Wait," Matt said. "Are you saying this is a guarantee? That every time I want to know God's will I should ask for a sign of encouragement and wait for it? That seems a little arrogant to me."

"Great question, Matt." Sam shook his head. "I'm not saying that at all. Of course there will be times when it doesn't happen. You have to tie this in with one of our key words: *relationship*. This is all about relating to a Father who loves us, who delights in us, and crawling up on his lap and telling him what we want. He always reserves the right to say no or remain silent."

Matt set his plate aside, picked up his Mead journal, and said to Sam, "So, give us the word, the verse, and the sentence." When Sam answered, he wrote, *Encouragement. Psalm 86:17. When you wonder if you're on the right path, ask God for a sign of encouragement.*

Lightning flashed in the night and a roll of thunder sounded in the distance. The young couple looked quickly at the old firefighter. Brenda riveted her eyes on him.

For a moment he continued to stare at the campfire. Then he leaned back and searched the eastern sky.

"Storm's still east of Kingfisher Ridge. But she'll be here before daybreak. We got our sign of encouragement today, and now God's asking us to weather the storm. When you say your prayers tonight, kids, you may want to ask the good Lord for a little rain to go with the thunder and lightning."

They went to bed. The dark lay heavy in the meadow under the clouded sky. From the distance there came the continuing report of thunder. Working from the light of her headlamp and the images on her camera screen, Brenda began to sketch out the scenes in her sketchbook. At the bottom of the drawing of the big buck in the meadow, she wrote Sam's word, verse, and sentence.

The storm from the east filled the tent with glorious light as the thunder rolled. Brenda looked down at Matt sleeping beside her, and his face was peaceful, for this day had unburdened him. And she remembered her morning prayer begging God to let her know that she was on the right path.

CHAPTER 7
TRIAL BY FIRE

Fools think their own way is right, but the wise listen to others.

PROVERBS 12:15

AROUND THE LITTLE morning fire where the coffeepot bubbled, the conversation centered on the weather. Brenda could feel Sam's concern more than see it. Late into the night the thunder had rumbled, nearing the edge of their meadow.

Sam scooped a handful of dirt and sifted it through his fingers. He sat on his heels and scanned the eastern sky. "Ground's powder-dry and the cloud cover's gone." His hand stopped working with the dirt. "Well, it's probably just as well. We'll hang here in Lost Trout Meadow and enjoy our next-to-last breakfast in the high country. Best not to move until the morning sun tells us what's going on. Once we know it's safe, we can work our way back to Casa."

Brenda watched Sam with fearful eyes, and she saw Matt

watching him too. With an attempt at measured discipline and control, she asked, "What do you mean when you say the morning sun will tell us what's going on?"

"Well," said Sam, "when lightning hits a tree in the night, the fire doesn't start to spread so you can see the smoke until the day heats up some. If there's a fire out there in these conditions, we'll know it soon enough."

Matt set his cup on the ground and swallowed. "I . . . I think we need a little more than that, Sam."

"I know. But you're going to have to listen. And I mean listen close like you're not used to, Matt. Listen in a way where you're not thinking for yourself but just taking in directions."

"I can listen like that."

"Of course you can. Well, kids—I mean, Matt and Brenda— I want you to look around here at this meadow grass, this brush, and these trees. How many times can they burn?"

"Once," said Matt. "They can only burn one time."

Sam motioned with his hand, sweeping right to left. "The safest place for a human being in a fire is the middle of the stuff that's already burned. If there's a fire coming our way, I'm going to lead you into the burn, into the black. The only way to get into the burn is to find a way around or sometimes through the flames. You're going to have to trust me enough to follow me into the burn. Can you remember that?"

"Trust you enough to follow you into the burn," Brenda repeated.

Sam nodded. "Trust me enough to follow me into the burn. Can you remember that, Matt?"

"Sure I can, Sam. Trust you enough to run into the burn."

"No! Trust me enough to *follow* me into the burn. Don't run anywhere unless I say run. But you can't waver when the time comes, because if you do, I can't help you." He rocked forward to his toes and stood slowly.

"I won't waver or argue, Sam. You're the expert up here," Matt acknowledged.

"Okay. I wouldn't worry too much. It's rare for a fire of any size to burn here. Let's get packed and ready for our trip to Casa. After the storm passes, it'll probably be a nice day on the plateau. Matt, maybe you can catch some more trout, and Brenda can sketch a little. I love the way you're planning to sketch a picture from our adventure to go with each of the eight sentences I'm teaching you."

Brenda stood and began walking toward the tent to retrieve her camera and sketchbook. Lightning flashed in the distance, and thunder exploded so loudly that she covered her ears. She twisted and looked to Sam for reassurance.

"I've been peeking over your shoulder some," he continued calmly. "You're a heck of an artist." He glanced again at the eastern sky and raised his cup to his mouth, draining it with his head back.

The three shared breakfast, struck camp, and stacked their backpacks against a tree. As the morning warmed the meadow, the shadows disappeared and Brenda thought the storm began to seem more distant. The forest waited in the sun.

Later in the morning, Matt and Brenda sat under the shade of a tree. Brenda was drawing in her sketchbook and watching the trout rise in a little pool when Sam walked over. "There's something I need to ask you."

Brenda smiled at him. "What's up, Sam?"

Sam was quiet for a long while. He put his hands in his pockets and looked down at his White's. "Matt and Brenda," he said at last, "I've only known you a few days, but they've been intense days. You may feel uncomfortable with this question, but I've got to ask it. Is there anything in me—I mean, in my behavior or the way I've treated you two; especially you, Brenda—anything you see that might help me understand how it is I hurt my Katie? If there's a kindness you could show me that would mean more than any other, it would be to tell me the truth. I can be a stubborn old man, and since Annie went on to heaven, I've been without the resource of her honesty and love."

Matt looked up, astonished. "You're asking us for advice?"

"No, I'm asking you for the truth about me. Advice and truth aren't the same thing. Advice is what you think someone should do. Truth is what you see them do."

Brenda coughed, hesitating. Then she took a breath and spoke. "Sam, you may be the wisest man I've ever met. But sometimes you can make me feel as if you care more about the point you're making than you care about me. Especially when you talk for a while like you're preaching a sermon, but then don't ask what I think. It's like you're trying to get away from me as a person while trying to get a principle into my heart. It doesn't work that way, Sam."

*

Sam stared at Brenda, but in his mind he saw his daughter, Katie, tearful and wounded, and that image carried him to memories dark and shameful. But Brenda's green eyes seemed to widen and deepen until they weren't the eyes of a student anymore but a friend's eyes, warm with compassion. "I'm so sorry, dear," he said. "There wasn't any intention in it. It was just cowardice on my part, making my point without giving you a chance to respond so I don't have to consider your reaction. I guess I'm regressing now that my Annie is gone.

"Matt, I'll ask again and then no more. Have you seen anything in me that might explain why I can't seem to get my Katie to trust my love again?"

Matt shook his head. "Sam, I don't feel comfortable with this conversation. Your relationship with your daughter is yours. I'm not a counselor, and obviously I haven't been that great at relationships myself. Brenda may have misspoken. We've only been up here with you for a few days. Sure, we've had our disagreements, but who am I to judge you?"

Sam took a step toward him. "You're a Christian, Matt. A newly born, re-created, Christ-in-you, Holy-Spirit-powered child of God," Sam said, clenching his jaw. "And I need you. Brenda didn't misspeak at all. She loved me with words I've never heard before. In all the years I've walked with God and all the friendships I've had in Christ, Brenda—your bride—is the first to connect my control of a conversation with my fear of risking what I can't control in intimacy."

Sam looked up for a moment and then back at the couple under the tree. "You're not the only ones trying to find some answers on this trip. There's a desperation in my heart," he said. "Like you feel when you wake up in the night knowing what happened yesterday but not knowing where you are at that moment. I'm having to dead-reckon myself back to my Katie. And I can't do it alone. I tried that for too long. Like the fool of Proverbs, I wouldn't listen."

Sam stood at the meadow's edge, absently considering the trees and his past. And then, with humble and hurting eyes, he looked at his two companions and his mind returned to the moment.

"In fact, this brings us to our next principle. Find a blank page in your sketchbook, Brenda, and write this one down. Before we leave this place, be sure to record this in your journal, Matt.

"The word is *community*, and the verse is Proverbs 12:15. I've memorized it, and you should too. 'Fools think their own way is right, but the wise listen to others.' The principle is simple: *Loners lose their way; trust the guidance of those who love you enough to tell you the truth.*"

Sam took off his hat and rubbed his right hand over his eyes.

He scratched his head, replaced his cap, and pointed to Matt. "I guess it's the most difficult lesson of all on discovering God's will," he said. "But if you want God to guide you, you have to open up and be known."

"I don't understand how that relates to finding God's will."

Sam nodded knowingly and was careful with his words. "If you hide who you really are from the ones God's called to tell you the truth, they can't protect and guide you with their love."

"I still don't understand."

"Careful, Matt. You'll get me to preaching again. It's a simple fact. Loners lose their way because they've cut themselves off from the truth the Holy Spirit wants to speak through others. They hide themselves from the blessing and the guidance of community."

"The Holy Spirit wants to speak through others." Brenda said the words under her breath, and Sam was glad she was mulling them over. But then she, too, looked confused. "I thought every Christian could hear from God. If he has anything to say to me about his will, he can just say it. Why would he trust others with his will for my life before he told me?"

"God knows that we're too sinful and stupid to find our own way," Sam said. "We come to Christ too broken, too manipulative, too afraid—and even after he's redeemed us, sometimes it's tough to tell what's really God's voice. Our own sinful natures get in the way. That's why he gave us community. I need you, and you need me. We have too many blind spots, too many pathologies. The Spirit's unwinding and healing those parts of our soul, and speaking truth through Christian community is one way he does that."

Matt came back at Sam as if they were discussing an accounting problem. "I actually agree with Brenda on this. If God knows me and speaks to me, then that should be enough. It seems like you're limiting God."

Sam stomped his left foot in the dirt, looked at his White's, and thought seriously of putting one of them up Matt's backside.

"You can't hide behind your theology and logic, Matt. I know. I tried it for years. I won all the arguments and lost my daughter." Sam sighed. "You keep telling yourself that you and God are enough, but someday you'll be living with the same regret in your heart that's killing me right now. Don't be a fool. There's your opinion, and then there's everyone else's. Be wise and listen."

Sam whirled and walked toward the packs. "Loners lose their way, Matt."

Brenda was yelling after him. "You're doing it, Sam. You're controlling the conversation."

Sam slowed and turned. "Do you see now why I need your help, Matt? Why I need community? I just hurt you in a way I wouldn't even be aware of if not for Brenda's courage. Maybe I'll never get better, but by telling me the truth, she's given me a shot at healing."

Suddenly Matt pointed to the eastern horizon.

"Fire!"

A plume of smoke and debris mushroomed thousands of feet above the trees. Its twisting coils of thick smoke and fire sucked air so violently that an anvil-shaped cloud was forming atop the plume. And it was moving toward them like a Texas thunderstorm, but it was hailing fire and brimstone.

"That's not just a fire. She's blowing up," Sam said.

Matt's voice burst hoarsely from his throat. "We're okay here in this meadow, aren't we, Sam?"

Sam smiled calmly. The trees bent west with the wind, and he turned to study the smoke plume. When he stood between them, the couple crowded near as if trying to draw from his strength. Sam was all business. "This is a full-on crown fire, meaning that it's in the trees and moving so fast it's creating its own weather. This meadow's too narrow. When it rolls through here, there's every chance that it'll spot across and both sides will go up together."

Matt suddenly came to life. "Spot across? What does that mean? You have to speak English to us here, Sam." He'd worked himself into a frenzy. "You have to be more clear."

"I'm sorry, Matt." Sam tried to explain. "The fire is going to hit this meadow with such force that embers will fly across to the preheated brush and trees on the other side, and more than likely this little meadow will become a fire trap."

Matt didn't answer, but he nodded slowly. His eyes stayed on Sam as he bent to tighten the laces of his broken-in boots. Brenda followed his lead.

Sam went on. "If you've never seen fire burn through timber, you have never seen combustion unleash its potential. Of course, we could stay here and risk it, but not with this fire weather. Not even a few seasoned firefighters in their shelters could survive what may be coming."

Again Matt nodded.

Sam took a deep breath. "Our only hope is to flank this fire and find some black to hunker down in—some smaller stuff we can run into that's already burned. It's about a half mile east to Big Dry Meadows. I'll take the lead," he said. "Matt, you bring up the rear. This meadow pinches closed about three hundred yards before the trail hits Big Dry. That means we'll be back in the trees for a minute. That will be the most dangerous time for us. If I tell you to drop your packs and run, just do it."

It seemed to take Matt some time to find his words. "We—follow you east," he said. "We drop our packs and run on your command."

"Drop your packs and run on my command," Sam repeated. "But be sure to stay with me, always east. Don't just panic and run. If it gets hot, you're going to want to run away from the heat to the south. That's sure death. Even that mulie buck on his best day isn't going to outrun this fire. You have to follow me into the burned-over area of Big Dry Meadows."

Sam stepped close to Brenda. "Remember, nothing in that pack's worth your life, sweetie. You have to do exactly what I say. Stay close to me."

Brenda nodded. "I'm ready," she said. "If you weren't here, we wouldn't have a chance. I'm afraid, Sam."

"I know," Sam said. "I know."

Matt turned toward the whoosh of a small stand of fir exploding as the forward finger of the main fire approached the meadow's edge. "It's here," he shouted. "Let's go! I can feel the heat from here."

Sam turned and walked over to the packs. He was stern now. "All right, you two," he said. "Hang on a minute." He pulled two oversize handkerchiefs from a side pouch of his own pack. "Here, tie these around your faces like an outlaw in a cowboy movie. It'll help you with the smoke."

"It's getting closer."

"Not as close as it's gonna get," Sam said. "Grab your packs, kids. Just follow me. Matt, don't run until I tell you to run."

"Yeah," said Brenda. "Sam's our only hope now."

They got in line. Sam started east across the meadow, then turned back to them. "God's our only hope. It's always the truth. We just feel it more intensely in a tight spot."

They kept moving. Matt stopped for a moment beside Brenda and they both looked at the smoke column marching toward them until Sam called, "Matt, Brenda! Stop staring at the fire and concentrate on following me."

Brenda half-ran to Sam's side. Matt moved slowly after them, and Sam recognized the heaviness of fear in his steps.

The sound of the fire grew deafening. The meadow was

darkening quickly in the shadow of the angry plume, and, above the trees, the smoke turned gray-black. Sam pushed harder and pulled his bandana up over his nose.

He turned his head left and looked off across the meadow and up at the flames, two hundred feet above the trees. The fire coming toward them in the ponderosa and fir stopped for a moment when it reached the grass, stalling like a runner taking a breath. Then the fire advanced weakly across the grass toward Lost Trout Creek. Sam had been listening for the lull. He shouted over his shoulder, "Get in front of me now, sweetie. I want to be between you and the heat. Look ahead where the trail hits the trees, Brenda. We're gonna make it to Big Dry."

Blocked by the creek, the grass fire stirred and swirled in dust devils of flame. Behind, in the trees, the main fire was loud and mean, with a sound like a freight train. "Okay, Brenda, run ahead now."

Brenda broke and started running along the trail. Sam shouted to her. "Stay on the trail. Keep moving. Trust me." He saw her looking down in the smoke, concentrating on the next few feet. Then she disappeared into the haze. Sam prayed she would soon be standing in Big Dry Meadows.

Sam spun, calling Matt to hurry up. An advancing finger of the main fire flared and sent embers sailing across the trail into the trees, starting spot fires. The sight of flames erupting in the brush and trees to the left and right froze the young man. Matt looked toward the place where Brenda had entered the trees, but he turned back.

Sam shouted through the smoke, walking toward Matt's indistinct figure. "No, Matt. This way. We're almost there."

"It's no good," Matt said. "We can't make it."

Sam caught up with him. He grabbed Matt's pack and wheeled him around. "Loners are losers, Matt. You have to trust me."

Matt jerked free, and the fire closed around them. Fear gripped Matt—Sam could see the terror in his eyes. "I'm going this way, Sam. It's my only chance."

Sam pulled him forward and slapped him hard in the face. He raised his arm again, and his hand shook.

Matt staggered and rocked backward. "Where's Brenda?" he cried, tears in his voice.

"Grab on to the back of my pack, son," Sam said tenderly. "And I'll take you to her. . . . She's just on the other side of these trees. . . . Trust me."

"I let you down, Sam."

"No," said Sam. "No, son. You didn't let me down. I just want to teach you to follow. That's all."

The roar of the fire got closer. Smoke columns twisted together through the manzanita and scrub pine, and several spot fires joined. Wind ripped flames high into the trees and sucked the oxygen from the trail.

Sam stepped aside and pushed Matt in front of him. "Run!"

Matt ran. He could feel the heat on the backs of his legs and wondered if that was why Sam didn't tell him to drop his pack. His lungs screamed for oxygen, but every breath drew in a mixture of heat and smoke. He pulled the bandana farther over his nose. From the edge of the trees he could see Big Dry Meadows for the first time. It was right there, just as Sam had promised. Where was the old man, anyway?

Waves of heat rolled over Matt as he stepped into the trees, and glowing pine and fir needles spun in the churning wind and ignited on his clothes. He lost the trail and stumbled over a root, catching himself in the dirt. With his nose down low, he realized he could get some air. *I'm not going to die on the ground,* Matt thought. *I am going to die trying to do exactly what Sam said: go into the burn!*

He took a deep breath, asking God to help him, and in adrenalized strength he jumped up and started pushing through the brush. He thrashed through a hell of dark smoke, superheated gases, and twisting winds. Suddenly he spotted an opening in the trees, and knowing that God had heard his cry, moved toward it. In the smoke and fire it was all that mattered.

Beyond the opening in the brush he could see the meadow, burned and black and inviting him to live. He remembered Sam saying it could only burn once. The roar of the fire intensified behind him, and the heat on the back of his legs and arms was so extreme he stopped thinking. His world reduced to the opening, the burn, and living.

He took one last giant fullback-like leap, backpack and all, through the burning brush and scrub pine at the meadow's edge, and landed on his pack. The force knocked the wind out of him, but he continued to roll away from the heat just as the superheated air ahead of the fire incinerated the trees behind him.

Matt stood and ran into the burned-out meadow. The air was clearing and his lungs were bursting. He took the biggest breath of his life, then dropped to his knees.

He shivered and became aware of Brenda pouring water from her Nalgene on smoldering hot spots on his legs and arms.

She shouted above the roar of the fire. "Get your pack off, Matt. Careful, honey. You have some burns on your shoulders."

An eerie stillness and an unnatural quiet filled Big Dry Meadows. With Brenda's help, Matt gingerly shrugged his pack to the scorched earth. A strange wind stirred, and wisps of smoke from the burned-over sage suddenly leaned horizontal. Matt could see and hear small pebbles flying toward the fire. He and Brenda turned toward a 747-like roar behind them, so deafening they instinctively covered their ears.

Flames and dark smoke whirled and roared as the main body of the fire hit Lost Trout Meadow, where they had camped the night before. As if in protest, the head of the fire rocked back and forth in the heat of the day. But then the smoke and flame began to spiral like a developing funnel cloud. In seconds the firestorm morphed into a huge tornado of fire and rage, rising high into the dry air. The devil wind spewed burning debris hundreds of feet into the sky and drove Matt and Brenda deeper into Big Dry Meadow.

They watched as smoke began to rise above the trees to their left. Mini fire whirls ignited in the brush, starting still more spot fires. And then the smoke columns on two sides of Lost Trout Creek merged thousands of feet in the afternoon sky. They coiled together, and the two-headed monster became one grotesque carnivore devouring trees, brush, grass, and animal life. The fires on each side of the Lost Trout pulled together and, creating weather, roared upward and turned west, a murderous tsunami of fire and smoke racing away from the couple standing in the safety of the Big Dry Meadows burn.

Matt and Brenda stood there, staring at the apocalyptic scene. Matt had noticed Brenda mechanically snapping picture after picture of the fire. He came slowly out of the layers of protection shock had put on his mind.

"It's just like Sam told us," Brenda said.

Matt looked down and back through the smoke and ash-white stubs of brush, and for the first time he realized how much time had really passed since Sam's push plunged him into the fiery brush.

The country around them seemed to heave a sigh of relief.

A mountain bluebird landed on Matt's pack, and quail began to call for one another in the distance.

But Matt stood stiffly and peered into the clearing smoke for any sign of life.

Brenda seemed to read his thoughts. She hurried to the charcoal edge of the tree line and looked back at Matt, then gazed into the moonlike landscape of the hell they had escaped.

"Where's Sam?"

CHAPTER 8

KEEP MOVING

We can make our plans, but the LORD determines our steps.

PROVERBS 16:9

THE FIRE BLEW WEST and north, and Big Dry Meadows yielded to its new reality: a landscape of black and gray rimmed by skeletons of burned trees and dotted with smoldering root pits and rats' nests. A muted auburn tint came to the skies. And the afternoon winds blowing through the ash stirred a fine dust that mixed with the smoke and lifted almost as high as the trees. The dead brush and fallen trees lay in Tinkertoy piles where the winds had pushed into the tree line, and flare-ups boiled. Along the scorched earth, flaming pinecones and twigs scrambled until they were halted and absorbed by some fiery stack of debris. Carcasses of squirrel, deer, and bear smoldered in the wind.

A mouse darted left and right through the black stubble,

swinging its tail from side to side, and ran to the shade of a sage that had somehow survived the fire. An opportunistic red-tailed hawk swooped in and gripped it by the neck, a whispering death that carried the mouse aloft while its little feet beat the air frantically, then stiffened.

Matt and Brenda stood alone in the meadow, staring through the haze toward the spot where they had last seen Sam. It was easy to make out the trail he'd led them to in the burned-over terrain.

The black meadow suddenly filled with the nonwilderness sounds of helicopter beats and low-flying aircraft. A plane appeared in the sky and dropped fire retardant on the western flank of the fire that burned along the ridge separating Lost Trout Creek from Nine-Mile Creek. A helicopter circled above Matt and Brenda.

Brenda cried out again. "When did you last see Sam? Matt, this isn't good. We have to find Sam."

"I don't think it's up to us to find Sam now, Bren. It looks like the people who know what they're doing just showed up." He took her hand and walked toward the helicopter that had landed a few hundred feet away.

Brenda leaned toward him. "Are you praying for Sam? I mean, if he's still alive?"

"Don't say that." Matt tried to make his words sharp and confident. "He's still alive. He has to be. Keep praying." He raised his eyes. "Lord, please help Sam."

A tall man stepped from the helicopter. He held his helmet under one arm while he stooped and ran under the whirling rotor blades. He wore green cargo pants and a long-sleeved yellow shirt. His fireman's helmet was coated in layers of a pink substance—some kind of fire retardant, Matt thought. The man moved with an assuredness that instantly made Matt feel more at ease. When he walked up to the couple, they both looked down at his boots—a scarred-over pair of White's, just like Sam's.

The firefighter held out his right hand to Matt. He gave a firm shake and looked intently from Matt to Brenda. "My name's Jack Nelson," he said, and his way was gentle. "Looks like you had quite an adventure up here. Are you okay?"

"There's an old man still in there. He didn't make it out," Matt said.

"All right. Tell me more about this old man. When and where did you last see him?"

Brenda was frantic. "He was right there." She pointed. "He saved our lives, but I don't know if he made it. His name is Sam, and he wore a pair of boots just like yours. He called them White's!"

Jack looked down at his own White's and pulled a radio from his belt. He studied the place in the charred trees Brenda had indicated. He kicked his left foot forward on its heel and pointed with his radio. "You say his name was Sam and he wore a pair of these," Jack confirmed. "That wouldn't be Sam Lewis, would it?"

"That's him," Brenda said. "We haven't seen him since he pushed my husband through the flames into this meadow. I don't know how anyone could survive the inferno he was standing in."

Matt had been following the conversation with his eyes. "I have a feeling he's still alive. Sam knows what he's doing up here."

Jack looked approvingly at Matt. He keyed the mike on his radio and reported the facts. He paused and looked left and right into the burn, then keyed his mike again. "The missing person is Sam . . . Sam Lewis. So let's get this right." His tone was insistent but calm. An encouraging volley of matter-of-fact 10-4s barked from the radio.

"If anyone could survive this tight spot, it would be ol' Sam," Jack said. "He's forgotten more about fire than the rest of us will ever know." He put his helmet on and twisted a bandana around his neck. "I'll get my copter in the air shortly, and there's a helitack crew on the way. I'll divert our resources to finding Sam. He's kind of a legend in these parts. Heck of a good man, too."

Matt saw something move out of the corner of his eye. He turned to find a familiar figure making its way through the smoke. "Sam!"

Sam entered the clearing, still in possession of his pack and hiking stick. Jack Nelson smiled. "Didn't I tell you ol' Sam would make it?" He keyed his radio again. "Disregard that missing-person report. Sam just walked out of the fire."

Sam dropped his pack next to Matt's and Brenda's, then squinted at them. "Good to see you two made it into the meadow. You did good, kids." He looked down and back up. "I mean . . . you did good . . . you two friends."

Brenda's face was bright with gratitude. "You saved us, Sam. I thought you were dead, but Matt wouldn't hear it."

Sam smiled at Matt and turned to Jack. The old man's face tightened and his lips pursed, as though an electric charge had hit a nerve.

"This here's Jack," Sam told Matt and Brenda, continuing on before Matt could say they'd already met. "He was the youngest fire management officer in the history of the US Forest Service. He can put out a small lightning fire involving one tree and supervise thousands of men and women battling wildfires of biblical proportions. But we've all called him Scaley ever since he was just a greenhorn." Having listed Jack's credentials— somewhat begrudgingly, from what Matt could tell—Sam turned to the firefighter. "Hey, Scaley, you got some cold drinks in that chopper? I sure could use one."

This time, in spite of the friendly words, Matt couldn't miss the uncharacteristically cold look in Sam's eyes and the shallow monotone in his voice. It was obvious that there was some history here.

Jack held out his hand and picked up the conversation as though he hadn't noticed the old man's manner. "You old buzzard. I got a mountain on fire here and you're asking for a drink?" There was a strange neediness in Jack's face as they shook hands. "Yeah, I'll get you a cold drink. How'd you manage in there, Sam?"

"You remember that little pool under the rocks south of the trail where we caught some nice trout on that backpacking trip?"

While Sam spoke, his face began to unbuckle. And by the time he paused for Jack's answer, the closed way between them appeared to have opened.

"I do," Jack said. "That where you hunkered down?"

"Yeah. After I pushed this young man toward the meadow, the wind got a little squirrelly." He smiled at Matt. "I knew I wouldn't make it, so I ran—and when I say *ran*, I mean I ran like an old man on adrenaline overload—and dove, or more accurately, fell down the bank of that pool. It got a little dicey, but I've seen worse. I'll be sore in the morning."

"Glad you made it out." Jack clapped a hand on Sam's shoulder, then bent and ran to his helicopter.

Sam's eyes were level and serious. "That was more of a lesson on community and trusting the truth from the people who love you than I meant to teach. It was close."

Matt stood in silence for a moment. "You love us, don't you, Sam?" he asked.

"You know I do." He took a step toward Brenda, and she threw her arms around his neck and cried.

Sam smiled and held her tight. "It's not my love for you that's on display here, kids. It's God's love for you and your love for him. These mountains show off his glory and majesty, but it's his guidance that shows off his grace and mercy."

Matt looked over at Sam and saw the calm, saintly eyes fastened on him. "Interesting," Matt said. "I used to scoff at sentences like that. I classified people like you as mystics trying to give God credit for everyday life. I enjoyed it. It made me feel smart and logical in comparison. But these last few days changed my mind." Matt shifted his voice, taking on a tone of declaration. "Why God put up with me I'll never know. But it does seem that he loves me in spite of my pride and stubbornness."

"It's not just you, Matt. It's me, and Brenda, too." Sam coughed smoke out of his lungs. "It's all of us. None of us deserve his guidance. He guides us because he loves us. Our responsibility is to just keep stumbling forward. He'll get us there . . . if we put one foot in front of the other."

Jack walked back over right then. He handed each of them a bottle of water from a plastic grocery bag. "Just like the Grand Fire in that last season before you went to seminary." He looked from Sam to the couple. "Those were Sam's exact words: 'One foot in front of the other.' I'll never forget it.

"Remember that night, Sam?" Jack said. His face was alight with the memory. "I can tell you two I'll never forget it. It was my first timber fire. We pulled into Road's End campground on the Kings River, and you could see the glow on top of the mountain. We'd been working all day, and the thought of hiking that steep trail had done us in.

"Ol' Sam was our superintendent, our crew boss, and he gathered us at the trailhead with our gear and asked us something." Jack's eyes were wide with the memory. "He said, 'Anyone know how we're going to get up this trail to that fire?'"

The old man shifted uncomfortably. "Hold it, Scaley. These kids aren't interested in old fire stories right now."

Brenda motioned with her hands for Jack to go on. "Nobody asked you, Sam. We kids—" she winked at Sam—"can decide for ourselves. Tell us more."

Jack sidestepped left, keeping an eye on the smoke rising above the horizon. "I remember thinking that he had some mountain-man secret to tell us." Jack took off his helmet and shook his head. "And then it came out: 'We're going to put one foot in front of the other. And next thing you know, we'll be there.'

"I was carrying that big ol' saw up those switchbacks all night long. Remember that beast, Sam?"

Sam chuckled. "Homelite 1020. Big felling saw I kept around that went out of production in the sixties. I remember the look on your face when I handed it to you."

"I can still hear your words echoing down that trail all night long," Jack continued. "'One foot in front of the other, boys. One foot in front of the other.'"

Matt had been staring intently at Jack. Suddenly the fireman's radio squawked, a request for instructions spoken over the *whump, whump, whump* of helicopter blades.

"Kernville Helitack. An H-523 is coming," Jack said.

Overhead, there was a burst of sound as a helicopter circled close.

Jack looked up slowly and with intention. "Sam, she's heading west and north. What do you think if I put the Kernville crew on the southwest flank and start firing from that ridge above Casa Vieja with air support to save the Nine-Mile drainage?"

Sam stepped back to let Jack turn toward his chopper. "That's what I'd do, son. But it's your fire. They'll need help when the winds shift if you want them to hold it." The old man paused in an attitude of respect. "You okay with us taking the Old Jordan Trail back around this mountain and camping in Casa tonight?"

Jack seemed to remember something for the first time. "Sure. Just don't stay at that little secret camp on the north side of the meadow you took me and Katie to that time. What do you call it—Honus Jonus camp?" He looked down at his boots and frowned. "Sorry to bring up Katie, Sam. Truly I am."

Jack glanced up apologetically and put his helmet on. "Just stay on the south side of Casa. It'll be a little noisy tonight. We've got crews walking in from the trailhead. Fulton's driving down from a fire north of here. They'll be coming through tonight, and I'm sure they're gonna want to say hey."

Sam was a long time in responding. "Guess . . . we need to talk about Katie . . . son. I think I should catch you up on things between my daughter and me. You knew she moved out east, and her practice is thriving from what I hear." He looked over the meadow. "But we're crossed, and she doesn't answer my calls."

Jack watched Sam's eyes. "Sorry to hear that, Sam." He paused, then assumed a more businesslike manner. "I need to get back to this fire. Our camp's setting up at Blackrock Station, and we're going to stage crews out of the campground there. You know how it is. But I'll have some time in the evening." He stepped closer to Sam, and then he looked down at his boots again. "We need to talk about this, Sam. You know I can't forget Katie, and there's never been another for me. I promise you I'm a different man than I was back then."

Sam nodded. "That's what I hear," he said. "Sorry we lost touch, son. I'm walking these kids out of here tomorrow morning and taking them to breakfast down at Nelda's in Lake Isabella. I'll drive back up tomorrow night and we'll visit."

Jack shook Sam's hand long and hard, and then the two of them walked toward the helicopter.

Brenda watched Matt questioningly. Matt twisted the top from his bottle of water. "Yeah," he said in response to her unspoken inquiry. "I heard that conversation, Brenda. I'll ask him."

"Jack and Katie?" Brenda cried with excitement.

"Let's saddle up, as Sam says. We need to start making our way back to Casa. Brian and Lindsey are expecting us to pick up the children tomorrow night."

Brenda didn't move. "You ask him right away, Matt, or I will, before we get all preoccupied with going home."

Matt helped Brenda with her pack, put on his own, and picked up the old man's. The two of them walked toward Jack and Sam. Just as they approached, Jack crawled into the helicopter and it took off.

Sam shouted above the noise. "Well, that worked out real nice. You learned the final lesson on finding God's will from the kid himself. *Put one foot in front of the other.* You're going to want to write that one down. The eighth word is *grace*. And the sentence is, *All is grace; put one foot in front of the other.* I got that one from Proverbs too."

The noises of aircraft chased toward the smoke in the northwestern sky. Matt and Brenda stood in the settling silence and stared at Sam.

"Just wonder if I could have offered that boy a little more grace." Sam's eyes were wet. "Not that I doubt my decision, not for one minute. No, sir." He stood still, sweat running down his face, and pushed his hands into his back pockets. "When you have responsibility for a child, you have to make some tough calls." He seemed to sort out this thought. "But that was the hardest one I ever made. And the most unpopular, too."

While Sam spoke, Brenda caught Matt's eyes, and he knew she wanted him to let Sam keep talking.

Sam defended his decision as if he'd been challenged. "Did you ever have the feeling you were missing something? Like others knew something you didn't—a missing piece of the puzzle you couldn't find? And then, when they said what it was, you knew that couldn't be it? Did you ever feel that way?"

Matt heard his own next sentence with amazement, hardly able to believe he was prying into Sam's family life. But it was out before he could stop it. "Jack and Katie were in love, weren't they?"

*

Sam sighed. This conversation had not been part of the plan for his mountain retreat with Matt and Brenda. "What am I doing talking to you kids about this? It's history now, and there's nothing I can do about it. Jack knew how I felt about him dropping out of USC to fight fire. He had a full-ride scholarship and could have made something out of himself. I told him, 'Katie deserves more than living in some godforsaken fire station and moving all over the country like I had to do.' She was starting med school then. It never would have worked."

Sam took his pack from Matt and swung it onto his back. "Jack wouldn't accept that. I said all he had to do was finish his degree. And then, if he still wanted to fight fire, he would have had options. But no, all he could think about was chasing fires around the mountain. It's a young man's game with no future. I should know. That's why I had to forbid him marrying my Katie. How was I to know he'd go back to college, get a degree in forestry, and become such a water-walker? Katie still thinks I stepped in because I have something against the boy."

He looked up at Jack's helicopter, heading toward the smoke in the distance. "That wasn't it at all. I'd seen too many Forest Service marriages go belly-up because of all the isolation, all the travel, all the hard culture. In so many ways Jack was the son I'd never had. But he was chasing windmills. I couldn't let a man like that—even a Christian man like that—marry my girl."

Sam thought suddenly of the only person who had ever made him feel this regretful over that decision. It was his Annie, with her kind face and her enchanting smile and her stunning green eyes that looked beyond his words into his soul.

He spoke softly, almost to himself. "I should have done it with a lot more grace. That's my main regret. I could have been a little softer on him . . . and her."

They stood alone in Big Dry Meadows and watched the air show. Planes and helicopters battled the fire from above, and the smoke billowed high and defiant into the sky. But Sam only felt the heat of Matt and Brenda's thoughts, burning with questions about Sam, Katie, and Jack.

He handed the map to Brenda and spoke gruffly. "Saddle up, friends. Here's where we are." He pointed to the place on the map. "We're going to want to dead-reckon to the southern end of Big Dry and over this ridge. There won't be any blazes on this hike, so pay attention to detail."

The three walked through the meadow toward the Old

Jordan Trail. They were coming to an unburned edge of the meadow where the towering pine and fir stood on each side of the path ahead. Sam could see the forested tops of ridges blue in the late afternoon.

Brenda abruptly hesitated at the trees. "The last time I followed a trail into the trees it didn't turn out too well."

"All is grace," Sam said. "You can't know what's out there. No one can know. I've faced a lot of tree lines in my life, Brenda. Not that I deserved to be loved and cared for by God, but I was. I just put one foot in front of the other—mistakes, regrets, failures, and all—and he led me along the way. And before I knew it, there I was. It's like the proverb says: 'We can make our plans, but the Lord determines our steps.' That's our last verse—Proverbs 16:9. We can look at it some more when we make camp tonight.

"So what I'm saying is this: I've come up with some terrible plans for my life, but the Lord has directed my steps. All is grace, Matt and Brenda. Just keep walking and trusting. All is grace; put one foot in front of the other."

Brenda gave him a trusting smile and stepped into the trees.

They walked on in silence for a time as Sam thought about how to illustrate his point. "The hardest tree line the Lord asked me to walk into was when I lost my dear Annie. She was the most compassionate person who ever lived. A light of kindness spread out from her. And all the colors of my world took on a shade of mercy. And the hard edges of my days softened. And the people in my life were good and noble. And I was not afraid to love."

"What did she think about you forbidding Katie's marriage to Jack?" Matt said.

Sam slowed and stood in silence on the lonely trail, tugged from his reverie. "She asked me to stay out of it," he said finally.

Matt turned and stepped toward him. "But you didn't. Because you don't really believe that all is grace, that you should put one foot in front of the other. Not when it comes to your daughter."

Sam neither moved nor looked up. "Jack was on the wrong path. Katie always wanted to be a surgeon, and he wanted her to settle for being a fireman's wife. I had to protect her."

"Protect her?" Matt countered. "You just told us that God is ordering our steps in spite of our lousy plans, and I want to believe you. But it's hard to accept when you refuse to believe that God could have been guiding your own daughter toward something you couldn't see. It's like you said to Brenda—nobody knows what's on the other side of the tree line but God. All is grace on both sides of the tree line, right? But not for Katie? You had to step in and help God because you were afraid of his guidance not working out the way you wanted it to for your daughter."

Sam snapped, "You're still young. Wait until your little girl thinks she's in love, and then we'll talk."

Matt was not put off. "That's your pride talking. Loners are losers, Sam. You wanted me to tell you the truth. Well here it is. When it comes to Katie, you're a hypocrite. No wonder she doesn't want anything to do with you. You can't trust God with your daughter. You didn't even trust your beloved Annie when it came to Katie."

Sam felt his eyes grow larger. What right did Matt have to confront him like this? But he had to admit the young man's words struck a nerve. Matt just didn't fully understand the situation. "Katie didn't know Jack like I did. He was stubborn and he wouldn't listen," Sam insisted.

Matt still wouldn't let it go, and his voice choked with emotion that surprised Sam. "Did Annie agree with what her father thought of you before she married you? And what if she didn't? Didn't she still deserve the chance to love the man you would become by God's grace, one step at a time? Either all is grace or it's not, Sam. You can't tell us to put one foot in front of the other when you won't do it yourself."

Sam closed his eyes. He spoke without pitch, without emphasis, and without any emotion, reciting perfectly logical words that had almost always convinced his own soul of the righteousness of his decision. "Jack wasn't making good choices. From the time she was a little girl, Katie planned to become a doctor. And I wasn't going to let her throw away that dream to marry some hotshot crewman."

Brenda entered the conversation, speaking for the first time since the tree line. "It's not just God you didn't trust. You wounded her, Sam. You hurt her little girl's heart because you didn't trust her. You made her choose between you and Jack, and she ended up losing both of you."

Brenda's words repeated themselves over and over in Sam's brain. *You made her choose between you and Jack.*

Sam looked sadly at her. Waves of pain surged through his body, leaving a numbness in his limbs and weakening his resolve. Katie was gone. It was just what his Annie had warned him would happen. There was a long pause, and then Sam said softly, "I lost her, didn't I?"

"Not yet, Sam." Matt put his hand on Sam's shoulder. "Dead-reckon your way back to her, my friend. All is grace; put one foot in front of the other."

Brenda spoke with a warmth and conviction that reminded him of Annie. "You have to take the first step toward her. Little girls can't handle it when Daddy walks away. And that's what you did, Sam. You stated the truth as you saw it and walked away."

Sam closed his eyes, tamping down his pride. He looked toward heaven and prayed aloud. "All is grace, Lord. I planned this trip to help these kids, but you directed my steps toward the truth I'm hearing from you right now through the two of them. I'm afraid of this tree line you're urging me into at this very moment. What if Katie doesn't want to see me? What if I say the wrong thing again? What if I just hurt her more? I'm telling you right now, Lord: I'll take that step toward my Katie. I'll dead-reckon and just keep moving, putting one foot in front of the other. Help me, please. Please have mercy on this old, stubborn soul and give me hope. In Jesus' name, amen."

Sam opened his eyes and looked fearfully to Brenda, then Matt. "Ain't that something? A few hours ago I walked through flame without fear. But right now I'm as scared as I've ever been."

Matt grabbed Sam's elbow. "Come on, Sam. We're too tired to try to dead-reckon to Casa by ourselves, and you're the only one who knows the way back. We're in this together. Brenda and I love you."

Sam let himself be turned and started down the trail. His voice was just above a whisper. "I know." He led them through the trees.

Brenda ran ahead and placed her camera on a rock just outside the tree cover when they reached the other side. "Stop there at the tree line." She framed the picture and set the timer, then rushed back to Matt and Sam. Sam stood between the couple with his arms around them and smiled for the first time since waving good-bye to Jack.

⚘

About nine that evening, Brenda sat by the fire ring with her sketchbook. She leaned against a log next to Matt as he helped her select sketches to go with each of the eight words and principles they had learned about finding God's will. This hunters' camp was on the safe side of Casa Vieja Meadow, and firefighters marched past on their way to the southwestern flank of the fire. It appeared to be the biggest news on the mountain that Sam Lewis had made camp here after surviving the blowup, and every crew felt the need to stop by for a visit.

As she flipped through her sketches, Brenda watched with amusement as Sam held court next to a table-like rock on the other side of the campfire, a cup of coffee in his hand. He warmly greeted starstruck young men, asking them about old friends. But as he'd informed Matt and Brenda earlier, Sam didn't want to hold these "greenhorns" up too much and violate his own convictions about small talk when there was a fire to put out. Every exchange ended with Sam making sure Fulton was still on the way.

"I hear Fulton's headed down from a fire to the north. They should be coming through anytime now, right?" Sam said to the latest visitor.

The old man's wide-eyed admirer filled him in. "Yeah, Mr. Lewis. Last time I heard them on the radio, they were turning up the hill from Limestone Campground."

"Heck, son. Mr. Lewis was my dad's name. It's Sam. Just plain ol' Sam."

Matt watched the firefighter walk away in the moonlight with the rest of his crew. "Who are these Fulton guys?"

Sam came around the fire and sat down next to him. "Fulton Hotshots, my old crew. One of the hardest decisions I ever made was giving up that crew to go to seminary." He smiled and stared at the flames before them. "But all is grace. One step at a time. And now here I am with a heart full of memories with people like you. Instead of dedicating my life to putting out fires on a mountain to save a few trees, I get to set fires in hearts to save this world from some of its hopelessness." And then he looked up at the stars. "And learn something about myself along the way. Now that's grace."

Sam's face lit up. "Speaking of fires in our hearts, I've got a surprise for you two tomorrow. The fire's way north of us now. We'll be able to walk out in the morning as scheduled. But you're going to have to follow me down to Lake Isabella. I want to take you to one of my favorite places for a mountain man's breakfast."

From right outside the camp came a voice. "Sam? Sam Lewis, is that you? Jack told me you were up here, you old son of a—"

Sam stood up and shouted, cutting the man off. "Well, Michael S. Morton! You forget yourself in front of my old crew? You're talking to a fireman-turned-preacher, young man. Let's show some respect for the lady here."

Brenda looked up. "That must be the Fulton Hotshots."

"This may take a while, Brenda and Matt. Remember, your word is *grace*. The sentence is simple: *All is grace; put one foot in front of the other.* The verse is Proverbs 16:9, 'We can make our plans, but the Lord determines our steps.'" Sam poured two cups of coffee. "Mike's the new superintendent of the Fulton Hotshots. His dad was a good hand and one of the best firemen I ever worked with. Got burned on a fire in Santa Barbara and the rest of us kind of raised the boy."

Brenda watched Sam walk away and smiled at his hurried pace. Michael Morton, now within sight, leaned on a shovel and took the hot coffee from Sam.

The campfire seemed reluctant to let go of its glow. It flared up warm and inviting long after it should have died down. Matt turned the pages of his notebook, and Brenda looked over his shoulder as they discussed their lessons on finding God's will and the biblical references Sam had given.

Trust. *God doesn't need your strength to guide you, but you do need to trust his strength to recognize his guidance.*

Proverbs 3:5-6—"Trust in the LORD with all your heart; do not depend on your own understanding. Seek his will in all you do, and he will show you which path to take."

Relationship. *Make sure you're all in for Jesus.*

Psalm 25:14 (NET)—"The LORD's loyal followers receive his guidance."

Intimacy. *Stay within the circle of intimacy with God, and trust him that you're on the dot of his good and perfect will.*

Psalm 139:23-24—"Search me, O God, and know my heart; test me and know my anxious thoughts. Point out anything in me that offends you, and lead me along the path of everlasting life."

Timing. *Live expectantly; God's signature on events is timing.*

Ecclesiastes 3:1—"For everything there is a season, a time for every activity under heaven."

Protection. *God's will is a flashlight, not a crystal ball; walk to the edge of the darkness and wait.*

Psalm 119:105—"Your word is a lamp to guide my feet and a light for my path."

Encouragement. *When you wonder if you're on the right path, ask God for a sign of encouragement.*

Psalm 86:17—"Send me a sign of your favor."

Community. *Loners lose their way; trust the guidance of those who love you enough to tell you the truth.*

Proverbs 12:15—"Fools think their own way is right, but the wise listen to others."

Grace. *All is grace; put one foot in front of the other.*

Proverbs 16:9—"We can make our plans, but the LORD determines our steps."

Brenda improved her pencil sketches of their favorite scenes to accompany each lesson and turned off her headlamp. They planned to make prints to give to Sam. "I'm ready for bed, Matt." Brenda yawned and laughed. "Sounds like Sam might be up all night. It's been quite a day. And you've been quite a man."

Matt looked up with happy weariness. His lips parted and his voice choked. Then he took a deep breath. He expelled the air slowly as tears spilled over his eyelids. His whispered words seemed to linger in the mountain air above the glow of the fire:

"All is grace!"

Brenda closed her sketchbook and studied the bright stars through the pine branches. She found the Big Dipper and the North Star. Across the meadow, a crew boss shouted orders to his team.

With her left hand she reached for Matt's right and pulled it into her lap. She clutched the sketchbook tightly to her chest with her other hand. "Put one foot in front of the other."

CHAPTER 9

BREAKFAST AT NELDA'S

IT WAS A CLEAR, gusty morning. The little mountain town of Lake Isabella, California, was waking up, and Forest Service rigs sat outside of Nelda's Diner. The mountains against the morning sky were the gold of grain, and the air was cool but dry. The morning wind had picked up and stirred the ash that had settled on the Kern River Valley from what was now being called the Long Canyon Fire. An old white Toyota Tacoma 4×4 turned left into the parking lot, followed closely by a stylish silver SUV manufactured in Europe.

They had walked out of Casa Vieja Meadow by headlamp in the predawn darkness, and Matt noticed that even the fire crews they met hiking downhill from the Blackrock trailhead didn't slow Sam's pace. "We need to be at Nelda's for breakfast.

I have a surprise for you kids." And he'd caught himself once again. "Excuse me. I have a surprise for you two . . . pilgrims."

As they followed the old man down the mountain roads to Kernville, headlights announced the approach of fire engines steering toward the blaze that still burned to the north. In the dark interior of their SUV, Matt and Brenda spoke softly. "Sam's pretty passionate about this surprise," Brenda said. She leaned over and rubbed Matt's right shoulder. "I wonder what this is all about?"

Matt concentrated on a sharp mountain curve, gripping the steering wheel tightly, and then he relaxed and patted her hand. "Only God knows, babe," he said. "And I mean that literally. I'm just trusting him for the next turn and as far as the headlights shine in the darkness."

Then he smiled and realized that he had applied one of Sam's maxims without even thinking. *God's will is a flashlight, not a crystal ball; walk to the edge of the darkness and wait.*

Brenda laughed. "Walk—or drive—to the edge of the darkness and wait . . . or keep driving until the next turn."

Matt knew he had learned useful truths from Sam about discovering God's will. He and Brenda were beginning to understand that the greatest obstacle to receiving God's will lay within themselves, and that only Christians who trusted his love enough to draw close to him and to one another would be able to recognize his guidance.

More important, Matt realized that God would change his

followers when they sincerely desired to know his will. Matt was not the same person who had driven up this mountain road just a few days before. He could only look back on his repentance and Brenda's forgiveness with a sense of profound gratitude and awe.

The light of imminent daybreak was growing brighter and brighter, and Matt stayed close to Sam's pickup as he wound around Lake Isabella and turned off Highway 178.

The knotty pine paneling inside Nelda's Diner was trimmed in the same red as the tables and counters, and the lamps hung high and bright over each booth. Locals sat on the stools at the counter, and teams of Forest Service workers and Kern County firefighters filled some of the booths. It was loud and clangy inside, and cooks and waitresses called back and forth through the open window separating the kitchen from the dining area. The smell of coffee and bacon and fresh-baked biscuits overwhelmed Matt with hunger.

A waitress hurried by with a coffeepot in one hand and a number of menus under her arm. She looked at Sam and winked. "Your friends are in the corner booth."

Sam looked pleased and smiled at Matt and Brenda. "Your surprise!"

In the back left corner under a hanging plant sat Brian and Lindsey. Brenda squealed like a schoolgirl and ran to her friends. Matt started to remind her that people were looking at her but caught himself. He smiled and slapped Sam on the back, then hurried after his bride.

After all five of them had settled into the booth, the waitress leaned over their table. "Coffee?"

Brenda looked up excitedly. "I'll have a French vanilla latte, please."

The sound of stifled laughter came from the firemen and locals within earshot. The waitress squinted her eyes. "This isn't LA, hon. It's coffee black or coffee with cream, sugar, or both. We don't do foo-foo up here."

"Just bring us some real cream and some sugar and sweetener," Sam said. "She'll be fine." The waitress sighed and filled their cups with coffee. Sam lifted his eyebrows and smiled at Brenda. "Mountain people have a bit of an attitude toward LA types."

Sam's attention seemed to drift away from them to the front of the diner. "Speaking of history, there's a couple of old buddies here I need to say hi to. I'll be right back. You all catch up."

Sam looked at Brian and Lindsey as he got up from the booth. "Thanks for driving up, you two. Matt and Brenda here have had quite an experience. An adventure of smoke and flame, just like the movies."

When Sam left with his coffee cup and started making his way across the diner, Matt picked up a menu and flipped through. The waitress arrived with the cream and sugar, and Brenda added both to her coffee.

Lindsey stirred sweetener into her own cup. "You know you made the news in Southern California. 'Southland Couple Trapped by Wildfire' was the headline on TV. It scared your children, but we kept telling them you'd be okay because we knew the man who was with you, and he wouldn't let you get hurt."

"I called them as soon as I could," Brenda said. "We talked this morning when we finally got cell service. They didn't give away your surprise." She smiled.

"They're great kids," Lindsey said. "And they can't wait for you to come home. Emma, our babysitter from church, is watching them today."

Matt said slowly, "The headlines were true. That wildfire did trap us. Sam saved our lives. But he was the one who almost got killed. You wouldn't believe the power of a crown fire." He sipped his coffee. "This has been a life changer for us. When you said you knew a guy, we never imagined what God had in store for us."

"What God had in store?" Brian repeated. He smiled and quickly looked out the window, then back. But before Matt could ask what he was doing, Brian said, "That doesn't sound like the Matt who sat with us in Walter's the other day."

Brenda gripped Matt's wrist firmly. "He's the same Matt—to me. Only better—better on the inside."

"That's true." Matt looked at the floor between his well-broken-in boots. "All is grace." He knew that if things had gone differently, if she hadn't forgiven him, Brenda might not even be sitting next to him right now. "Did Sam teach you that one?"

"Of course he did," Brian said. "Maybe that was the whole point of God bringing Sam into our lives." Brian took a swallow of coffee and set down the cup. "I wish my family had heard this principle when I was a boy. We didn't seem to view finding God's will as an exercise of grace at all, and it was almost too late for me . . . until I met Sam."

That surprised Matt because he'd always thought Brian was fortunate to be from a well-known Christian home.

"You're serious?" Brenda asked.

"Brian used to be so performance-driven when it came to his relationship with God," Lindsey said. "He talked about God's mystical ways, but until Sam bored into his pathological need to perform, he just couldn't believe that God would guide him in spite of his failures. You should have been there that night in Kern Flat when Brian broke down and accepted God's love. He wept for hours. It was the most dramatic movement of the Spirit I've ever seen in a man."

Matt was confused. "You turned left out of Casa Vieja?"

"Of course," Brian said. "You didn't turn right, did you?"

Brenda set her palms on the table. "What does it matter? I saw a pretty spectacular movement of the Spirit in my man too. That's what happens when people spend time with Sam in the high country!"

Matt looked at Brian and spoke from his heart. "That first lesson—that God doesn't need my strength to guide me, but I need to trust his strength to recognize his guidance—was the beginning of healing in me. I resisted it as long as I could. But Sam laid me open with his truth and love." He stared at his coffee. "I may not have received a direct answer about whether we should move to Pasadena, but God changed me. He changed us. He saved our marriage." Matt put an arm around Brenda. "I think he's just now revealing his purpose in sending us on that retreat."

Brian followed Sam with his eyes as the old man worked the room. "If it weren't for meeting that man, I hate to imagine where we'd be today."

Brenda agreed. "I wish there were something we could do for him."

"There is," Lindsey whispered. "Did he tell you about his heartache over his daughter, Katie?"

Matt whispered too, though he wasn't sure why. "Yes. And I got in his face some over that. I found myself repeating his own advice to him." Matt sat up and took a deep breath. "That was the day he saved us from the fire, and I felt a little awkward. But I know it was what he needed to hear."

They ordered breakfast when the waitress returned. "Well, I don't know what you said to Sam about his daughter," Brian said. "But I suspect it was what Lindsey and I have been thinking."

Lindsey leaned in. "Sam thinks he brought you here to surprise you. We have a bigger surprise for old Sam."

Sam returned with an empty cup. "Well, Matt and Brenda, is this a sign of encouragement or what? Did you tell them about your close call? Your trial by fire?" He waved at the waitress and she returned to fill their cups and take Sam's breakfast order.

"I'll never forget that," said Brenda. She put her elbows on the table and scrolled through the scenes on her camera screen. "Here are some pictures of the fire."

The waitress brought a tray of food, and over their mountain breakfasts, the five friends laughed and reviewed their personal experiences with Sam's eight principles.

When there was a lull in conversation, Sam looked around the table. "These teachings work in your lives because you're devoted followers of Christ. Only those who are all in for Jesus recognize God's guidance. This is what I want to do with my life: help young people like you find their way. Even if I lost my way with my own daughter."

"Sam, it's not too late for you and Katie," Brenda said. "Remember what you said? 'Live expectantly; God's signature on events is timing.'"

Matt saw a terrible sadness come to Sam's eyes. The older man closed them and kept them closed. A wrinkle formed between his brows. "What I'm trying to say is that you four are God's answer to my desperate prayer to give my life meaning and my heart hope."

Lindsey reached for Sam's hand. "Sam, you're not alone in this. Will you trust our love for you and God's timing?"

Matt glanced up, for someone had just stopped beside their table. A young woman was standing there, looking down at Sam. She was beautiful and dignified. She had kind, wide-spaced green eyes. Her simple but elegant blonde hair hung to her shoulders, and she wore jeans, hiking boots, and a cotton top.

"Daddy," she said, gazing at Sam.

An absolute silence settled on Nelda's Diner. The firefighters put their forks down and stared. The waitress froze her coffee-pot over a waiting cup at the next table and looked up slowly.

Sam's eyes opened, looked for the voice, and finally found the young woman's face. "Katie," he said. "But how? Who?"

Sam stood up quickly, without decorum, and bumped his knee violently on the table. Coffee spilled from all five cups. He took two steps and grabbed his daughter, pulled her close, and held her.

Outside, there was a burst of sound as a California Division of Forestry fire engine screamed by with its siren blaring.

Matt watched with a fearful excitement. Katie melted into her father's arms and patted him on the back. They held each other for much more than a moment. She pulled back and held his face in her hands. "I've missed you, Daddy."

Sam stepped away and placed his hands on her shoulders. Competing waves of regret and thanksgiving crashed over his face and spilled tears down both cheeks. But he smiled at Katie through the tears. "I'm so sorry," he said. "How did you know I would be here at Nelda's?"

She twisted toward the table and patted her father's cheek softly. "Which one of you is Brian?" she asked.

Brian raised his hand, and Katie pointed at him. "Brian

talked me into coming, and he and Lindsey bought the ticket. I drove up from LAX last night."

"We're paying for half of that ticket," Brenda interrupted.

Sam said tonelessly, "I was afraid I'd never see you again— ever." He smiled in sudden shyness but then turned to his four students. "Kids, let me tell you something about myself that Katie already knows." His voice gained tone and texture. "I'm independent when it comes to finances. I pay my way. I'm a mountain man, and that's what we do up here. We pay our way."

Katie's shoulders dropped and her smile faded. She looked around Nelda's and said, "Let's sit down, Dad."

The change in her demeanor and the transition from *Daddy* to *Dad* wasn't lost on Matt as he and Brenda moved right to make room for Katie. Sam took his seat next to Brian and Lindsey.

"Dad, if you won't let them pay for my ticket, at least let me. I'm a surgeon, and I don't have one worry when it comes to finances. You're not in a place to spend money like that."

"Nonsense. It's our treat and the least—" Brian began.

"I won't hear of it!" Sam's voice was stubborn, and he spoke with narrowed eyes and brows pushed low together. He moved his head forward, glared around the table, and took a drink of hot coffee. "I don't take charity. It's settled."

Lindsey's face went obstinate. "You just stepped out, Sam, you stubborn old fool."

"Stepped out of what?" Sam snapped.

"Stepped out of the circle of intimacy with God and us—and out of his will," she said softly, her voice certain.

Brenda was leafing through her sketchbook. "Here it is, right here under my sketch of you hunched over the circle and the dot with that stick at Honus Jonus camp."

"Honus Jonus camp?" Katie asked. "Did it burn?"

Sam reassured her, looking into his coffee cup. "No, Katie. Scaley's the incident commander, and he wasn't going to let that place burn."

❧

Sam's forefinger rimmed his cup for a moment and then slowly fell to the spoon on the table and pushed it back and forth. He knew Katie was looking at him. He could even picture in his mind, without looking up, how hopeful her expression would be at the mention of Jack Nelson. His thoughts raced like a child trying to outrun the foam of the surf on a beach. He raised his head and regarded her, and his mental picture had been precise.

Brenda spoke. "First let me read one of our Scriptures to you, Sam. Psalm 139:23-24. 'Search me, O God, and know my heart; test me and know my anxious thoughts. Point out anything in me that offends you, and lead me along the path of everlasting life.'"

When Matt spoke, Sam saw Katie jump at his intensity. "Listen, Sam. These are your words, not ours, but they're true."

He leaned over the table and focused on Sam's eyes. "'Stay within the circle of intimacy with God, and trust him that you're on the dot of his good and perfect will.' At this very moment God's probing your thoughts through us, and we all agree that your mountain-man pride seems to be an idol. You are decidedly not in the circle of God's revealed will for your life."

Sam watched Katie closely, and her shoulders relaxed as she leaned back against the leather booth. She looked from face to face of the other young people, seemingly astounded that they were actually standing up to her father. He felt the same way.

Lindsey reached around Brian and touched the back of Sam's hand with manicured fingers. He stared at the soft circles her fingers rubbed on his scarred and grizzled hand.

"My father was a proud man too, Sam," Lindsey began. "He refused to let Brian pick up the check, even though we made three times his salary. But that was just the tip of his pride iceberg. Under the surface was a mountain of hurt that never healed in my heart. And there were so many times I sat right where your little girl sits now, wondering if anyone would ever speak up so we could have a chance at intimacy. This is your opportunity to step back into the circle. Not only the circle of intimacy with your heavenly Father but the intimacy you told us you longed for—intimacy with your daughter, your Katie."

Katie's shoulders shook as she cried silently. She reached for her napkin and wiped her eyes. "I'm sorry. It's just that—"

Brian smiled at her. "You're okay," he said. "This is a moment we can't waste. A perfectly timed moment from God."

"God's signature on events is timing," Matt interrupted. "And this is your time, Sam. Time to trust his strength, time to make sure you're all in for Jesus, time to step back into the circle, time to find the dot of his good and perfect will for you, time to walk to the edge of the darkness and wait, time to trust the guidance of those of us who love you enough to tell you the truth, and . . . time to put one foot in front of the other."

"Let us pay for the ticket, Sam," Lindsey encouraged him. "That's your next step, your trust step, your God's-will-for-you step. Let us pay for the ticket. Then wait at the edge of the darkness of your pride and fears."

"And we're covering breakfast, also," Matt added.

"You can pay for breakfast and the ticket, too," Sam whispered hoarsely. "I know I've wounded her." He took Katie's hands. "I've wounded you, my sweetie. I've wounded you with my stupid mountain-man pride. How will you ever forgive me?"

Sam's mind wobbled between anger at himself and love for those seated around this table. And then he regained his voice with passion and affection. "If I'm being honest . . . Why not just say it and grieve the reality? Aside from Annie, nobody's ever loved me and Katie the way you kids just now loved us. You loved us with the truth, a truth I don't know exactly what to do with." But then he realized what to do. *Trust their love completely. Don't hold back anything. Don't try to control anything.*

Just trust, and walk to the edge of the darkness and wait. Give Katie a chance to be the woman of God you raised her to be. And maybe give Scaley the opportunity to be the man he wants to be. Why not? He jumped up, took Katie's hand again, and said to his friends, "There's something I have to talk about with my little girl."

✿

The four flatlanders gazed out the window, watching father and daughter walk out of Nelda's. Sam pulled down the tailgate of his pickup, and he and Katie sat together and talked.

Matt spoke solemnly. "The high country humbles a man."

"All is grace," Brenda said.

And the four friends looked at one another and agreed. "All is grace."

DISCUSSION QUESTIONS

1. Matt and Brenda represent two perspectives on how to discover God's will. Matt takes a commonsense view: "Just read your Bible, consider your options, and make the most reasonable choice." Brenda embraces a more mystical method: "God guides through circumstances, feelings, and signs." Which way do you lean, and why? What are the potential downsides of each?

2. According to Sam, "If you want to experience God's guidance, you must go beyond understanding to trust" (page 15). How does Proverbs 3:5-6 support that advice? Describe a time when you relied on your own understanding and strength to make a decision. What happened?

3. In what area of your life (marriage, children, career, finances, relationships, etc.) do you struggle most to trust God? How does this affect your capacity to hear God's guidance in that area?

4. When Matt doesn't listen to Sam's advice on where to set up camp, he witnesses the potentially disastrous consequences. What kinds of dangers do we face when we don't trust God enough to recognize his guidance?

5. Sam believes that "90 percent of knowing God's will is staying within the circle of intimacy by genuinely opening our lives up to his examining Spirit" (page 53). *In what ways are you opening up your life to God? In what ways are you still holding back?*

6. Why is it important that we affirm God's omniscient love and invite him to examine our hearts before we plead for guidance?

7. Picture the circle and dot Sam scribbled in the dirt. When have you felt like you were out of the circle? What needed to happen for you to get back in the circle of God's will? Why is it important to make sure you're in the circle before you start looking for the dot?

8. In your own life, where have you seen God's timing in an unexpected or unwelcome event? Can you now look back and recognize God's love in that experience? Why or why not?

9. How does God use the Bible to guide Christians? In what way will knowing the Bible help you keep moving on the path God has prepared for you?

10. In chapter 6, Sam prays for a sign of encouragement. Have you ever experienced a sign of encouragement from God during a hard time? What did that look like?

11. Brenda lists several signs she's noticed—for example, "how the light shining on a painting in a doctor's office looked like a cross, so she knew that was God's doctor for her." In response Sam tells her, "There's a fine line between a sign from God and superstition" (page 126). What are the hazards of viewing almost any circumstance of life as a sign from God? How can we guard against this tendency? On the other hand, what are the risks of deciding that you'll never receive a guiding sign from your heavenly Father?

12. In chapter 7, Matt and Brenda don't understand why community is often necessary for Christians to discern God's leading. Why is opening our lives to others a particularly difficult step for many Christians to take? Can you think of a time in your life when someone was courageous enough to tell you the truth and it saved you from making a mistake?

13. Which of Sam's principles for discovering God's will is most difficult for you to apply? Why?

14. How can these principles help you make decisions as you walk with Christ?

ACKNOWLEDGMENTS

Thanks to . . .

The Fulton Hotshot crew I fought fire with for seven years of my youth.

Dale Dague and Mike Martin, who introduced me to the high country and shared so many of the lessons of life dramatized in this book.

Denise Christensen McCormick, Mandy Ray, and Aimee Ronnow, whose perceptive comments caused me to rewrite this book more times than I wanted, but the number of times it needed.

The team at D. C. Jacobson & Associates, who were the first to believe in this book.

Tyndale House Publishers, for their careful stewardship of the manuscript through Jon Farrar's excellent leadership and Danika King's skilled editing.

My faith community, Church of the Open Door, that loves me well.

My bride, Judy, whose love brings color to my life.

And to you, the reader, for your longing to discover God's will. May God give you unshakable confidence that you're on the right path.

ABOUT THE AUTHOR

ED UNDERWOOD is a pastor, an author, and a speaker. In addition to leading Church of the Open Door in Southern California, Ed has taught Bible school students and seminarians, spoken to packed conferences, and written numerous articles and books. When Ed is not studying, leading, discipling, writing, or speaking, he loves spending time with his wife, Judy, and their children and grandchildren. He enjoys backpacking and still tries to surf some.